....
....
....

——————

West Bend Community Memorial Library
West Bend, Wisconsin

DEMCO

WE THE PEOPLE

WE THE PEOPLE

The Story of the
United States Constitution
Since 1787

Doris Faber and Harold Faber

CHARLES SCRIBNER'S SONS • NEW YORK

Charles Scribner's Sons Books for Young Readers
Macmillan Publishing Company
866 Third Avenue, New York, NY 10022
Collier Macmillan Canada, Inc.

Printed in the United States of America
First Edition
10 9 8 7 6 5 4 3 2 1

Library of Congress Cataloging-in-Publication Data
Faber, Doris, 1924–   We the people.
Bibliography: p.
Includes index.
Summary: Discusses the changes in the Constitution since the original document was signed in 1787 and how they came about.
1. United States—Constitutional history— Juvenile literature.
[1. United States— Constitutional history]
I. Faber, Harold.   II. Title.
KF4541.Z9F33   1987   342.73′029   86-31404
ISBN 0-684-18753-1   347.30229

Contents

Preface

Every year, millions of Americans come to see Indepen dence Hall in Philadelphia. It is a handsome old building of red brick, a fitting birthplace for the United States. Here the Declaration of Independence was adopted in 1776, and here, eleven years later, the Constitution—still the supreme law of the land—was written.

Two hundred years afterward, visitors are hushed as a National Park Service guide takes them into the reconstructed chamber where delegates to the Constitutional Convention met throughout the hot summer of 1787. On a dais at one end is the chair in which George Washington presided as chairman of the convention. Close to a railing is Benjamin Franklin's chair. In front is the desk where James Madison sat, taking notes of all the proceedings.

But it requires another trip, to Washington, D.C., to view the actual document they and thirty-six other delegates signed on September 17, 1787. The original Constitution, written in ink on parchment, is on permanent display at the National Archives Building in the nation's capital. It rests in a case enclosed by special glass to filter out light that might damage the faded ink, surrounded by inert gases to protect the parchment against deterioration. It sinks into a basement vault at night to protect it against vandalism or theft.

Seeing Independence Hall or the Constitution itself gives most visitors a solemn feeling. Suddenly, the founding fathers of the United States seem no mere marble statues, but real people.

A drawing of Independence Hall made in 1778 when it was still known as the Pennsylvania State House. *Courtesy Independence National Historical Park*

The rotunda of the National Archives Building in Washington, where the Constitution adopted in 1787 is on permanent display. *Courtesy National Archives*

Who were they? What did they say to one another? How did they achieve that "miracle at Philadelphia," as the Constitution has been called? How has it survived and changed over the past 200 years? That is the story to be told in the pages that follow.

WE THE PEOPLE

1

A Call to Duty

BECAUSE GEORGE WASHINGTON KEPT A DIARY, we know just how he occupied himself during the spring of 1787. He recorded his every horseback ride out to supervise the plowing of specific fields comprising his Mount Vernon plantation, besides noting whenever he went fishing or welcomed company for dinner. But the father of our country was not the sort of man who wrote down much about his own feelings.

So we have to guess what he felt upon once more being summoned away from his home. That spring, Washington was chosen by the Virginia legislature to be one of the state's delegates at a new Federal Convention in Philadelphia. The meeting had been called to revise the Articles of Confederation, under which the thirteen former British colonies along the Atlantic seacoast were only loosely tied together as the United States.

Judging from letters Washington sent several of his

friends, it is obvious that he hesitated over whether to go to Philadelphia. Could anything positive be expected to come of any such assembly? If he had decided against making the trip, of course American history would have turned out quite differently.

Yet Washington was already the young nation's great hero, owing to his leadership of the Continental Army in the Revolutionary War. It would not be too much to say that he personally had become the main unifying force among otherwise divisive factions in the various states. Despite his extreme reserve—nobody has ever portrayed him smiling—the solemn dignity of this tall, ruddy-faced man must have been very reassuring. And although he often expressed his opinions ponderously, his words reflected a high-minded common sense that inspired much trust.

Still, in 1787, Washington had reached the age of fifty-five, and he thought he would never again "take any part in public business." Four years earlier, he had returned to Mount Vernon after being absent for eight years, leading the American forces to victory over the British. More openly than usual, he had described his own outlook in a letter to the young Marquis de Lafayette, one of his aides during the war:

> At length I am become a private citizen on the banks of the Potomac, solacing myself with tranquil enjoyments, retiring within myself, able to tread the paths of private life with heartfelt satisfaction, envious of none, determined to be pleased with all and, this being the order for my march, I will move gently down the stream of life until I sleep with my fathers.

Washington had a tremendous sense of duty, however, and a number of men he respected did their best to convince him

George Washington as seen in a painting around 1787. *Courtesy Independence National Historical Park*

that his presence in Philadelphia was essential. A letter from James Madison told him: "It was the opinion of every judicious friend whom I consulted that your name could not be spared from the deputation to the meeting in May in Philadelphia." Washington's old war companion General Henry Knox wrote: "Your attendance would confer upon the assembly a national complexion, and more than any other . . . induce a compliance with the measures of the convention."

As a result, Washington decided that, in good conscience, he could not stay home. Shortly after sunrise on the morning of May 9, 1787, he bade farewell to his wife, Martha, then climbed into his carriage. Accompanying him on what was a long journey in those days were a servant and a groom for his horses.

A week's trip over rugged dirt roads and across rivers on rude ferries brought Washington to the town of Chester, Pennsylvania. There he was met by some of his Revolutionary War colleagues, including General Knox. They accompanied him on one more ferry crossing—to a gala ceremony planned by the citizens of Philadelphia to greet him.

As church bells rang and artillery boomed, Washington was escorted into Philadelphia by a troop of cavalry smartly turned out in white breeches, high-topped boots, and round black hats decorated with silver. There were resounding cheers from the people lining the streets of what was then the largest city on the North American continent. With a population of 40,000, Philadelphia was a center of commerce, shipping, science, politics, and art, even boasting some paved sidewalks that were lighted at night.

Washington climbed down from his carriage at a rooming house on Market Street, one of the best local accommodations for travelers of his day. But, as he wrote in his diary that evening, "being warmly and kindly pressed by Mr. and

Mrs. Robert Morris to lodge with them," he changed his mind and moved into their home.

Morris, who had been superintendent of finance for the Continental Congress during the later years of the Revolutionary War, was a rich man. His three-story brick residence was lavishly and comfortably furnished. It had many bedrooms, an icehouse for chilling summer drinks, a hothouse for growing exotic fruits, and stables for twelve horses.

As soon as he was settled in the Morris house, Washington paid a courtesy call upon Benjamin Franklin, the eighty-one-year-old scientist, philosopher, and diplomat who was Pennsylvania's most distinguished citizen. Only two years earlier, Franklin had returned home to America after many years in Paris, making friends for the rebellious colonies and negotiating a peace treaty with England. Now he was president of the Pennsylvania Assembly, a post equivalent to that of governor of the state.

The two most illustrious citizens of the United States could not have presented more of a contrast. The austere Washington stood over six feet tall, with the upright bearing of a military commander. Franklin struck a visitor of the time as "a short, old, fat man in plain Quaker dress, bald pate, white locks," with some of his grandchildren constantly about him while he sat in his garden. As the highest official in Pennsylvania, Franklin was host to the delegates to the new Federal Convention, and most of them paid a call on him.

He delighted to show his visitors his new find, a two-headed snake just caught near the confluence of the Schuylkill and Delaware Rivers—a creature about ten inches long, with the heads joined just below the jaws. What would happen when the snake was traveling on the ground among bushes if one head wanted to go in one direction and the

Benjamin Franklin as depicted by the noted artist C.W. Peale.
Courtesy American Philosophical Society

other in a different way, with neither consenting to go back
or give way to the other? Franklin wondered aloud whether
delegates to the convention might in some way be comparable. For unless the various delegates agreed to go in the
same direction, they scarcely could be expected to accomplish much.

Symbolically, the meeting between Franklin and Washington marked the beginning of the Federal Convention. Without their presence, the convention could not succeed. Without their approval, any changes recommended by the convention would not be supported by the people. There is no record of what the two men said to each other on that occasion, but undoubtedly they talked about the task confronting them.

The nub of the problem was how to govern the new nation. It consisted of thirteen states, which had united for the purpose of winning independence from England. But with independence won, they were jealous of their own rights and powers. They had united for war, but could they remain united in peace?

Together on June 16, 1775, they had agreed to the appointment of Washington as commander of the ragged Continental Army. Together on July 4, 1776, they had adopted the Declaration of Independence. Together on November 5, 1777, in the Continental Congress, they had consented to unite under the Articles of Confederation.

But the Articles provided only a Congress, in which each state had equal representation and vote. Nine votes of the thirteen were necessary before any major action could be taken. There was no chief executive, or president, as we know the office today. There was no federal court system. The Continental Congress had no power to tax, raise troops, regulate commerce, or enforce its own laws. Those powers belonged to the individual states. So, by 1785, the government of the United States was "a wheedling beggar," according to the historian Clinton Rossiter.

The weaknesses of the confederation were apparent to all. Even before the Revolutionary War had ended, committees had been appointed to recommend changes in the Articles, but they could be amended only by the unanimous vote of all the states. That was most unlikely to happen because the small states, which had an equal vote, were suspicious of any plan that might give more power to the larger states.

Yet times were changing. The Revolutionary War had brought the emergence of a new kind of citizen, one who paid allegiance to the United States as well as his own state. Despite different patterns of speech and customs, the new Americans shared a common hope for "life, liberty, and the pursuit of happiness." The experiences of war had welded together many thinking citizens of the new world who had come to the conclusion, as Franklin put it, that "united we stand, divided we fall."

Washington himself, in letters to his friends, made no secret of his own belief that a stronger union was necessary. To one, he wrote: "We are either a united people under one head, and for federal purposes; or we are thirteen independent sovereignties, eternally counter-acting each other." He told another: "The discerning part of the community have long since seen the necessity of giving adequate powers to Congress for national purposes. . . ."

With that background, the move toward the great Federal Convention of 1787 had begun at a meeting between representatives of Virginia and Maryland in 1785 to resolve a quarrel about navigation on the Potomac River. They agreed to a system of commercial regulation, but their major contribution was to invite the other states to another meeting, this one to be held in Annapolis, Maryland, in 1786.

It was in Annapolis that the two brilliant strategists of a new form of federal government—Alexander Hamilton of New York and James Madison of Virginia—came together. Unlike as they were in background and experience, both of

Alexander Hamilton around the time of the Constitutional Convention. *Courtesy Independence National Historical Park*

these young men shared the conviction that the United States could survive only with a national government possessing sufficient powers actually to govern it.

Hamilton was only thirty-one years old, an awesomely

able but rather snobbish lawyer. Born on the island of Nevis in the West Indies, he had served as an aide to Washington during the Revolution, reaching the rank of colonel. From his wartime experience in the ill-equipped army that frequently went unpaid because the Congress had no money, Hamilton had reached the conclusion that a federal government with a strong executive and a sound money system was imperative.

Madison had come to the same conclusion a different way, as a serious student of the theory and history of government. Thirty-five years old, he was not much more than five feet tall and weighed only about a hundred pounds—no bigger than "a half piece of soap," someone said. But his mental stature had made him a member of Virginia's assembly that framed the first state constitution, as well as a representative in the Continental Congress. There, despite his quiet manner, his mind won him an increasing influence. Because of the pressure he kept exerting in favor of adopting a more effective national charter, he would often be called "the father of the Constitution."

Still, only five states—New York, New Jersey, Pennsylvania, Delaware, and Virginia—sent delegates to Annapolis. Other delegations were either not appointed or failed to attend. Those present adopted a resolution, drafted by Hamilton, calling the condition of the nation so critical that each of the thirteen states should appoint commissioners to meet in May of 1787 in Philadelphia to "devise further provisions as shall appear to them necessary to render the constitution of the Federal Government adequate to the exigencies of the Union."

In that year of 1786, the thirteen states were divided by conflicting trade interests and policies. Some thought that

James Madison, often called "the father of the Constitution."
Courtesy Independence National Historical Park

the divergent interests of the North, with its shipping and
fishing trade, and the South, based on a plantation economy
and slavery, called for the division of the states into two separate nations. Benjamin Rush of Philadelphia, a physician

who was also a noted patriot, even wondered whether the former colonies should be divided into three nations—"an Eastern, Middle and Southern Confederacy."

But a more fearsome specter—rebellion—confronted the states that had won their independence by a successful rebellion against England. In 1786, desperate farmers in western Massachusetts, angry at seizures of their land and cattle because of their inability to pay taxes, petitioned the state legislature to halt foreclosures on their property and to prevent imprisonment for debt. After the state failed to act, the farmers rose in armed protest under the leadership of Daniel Shays, who had been a captain in the Revolutionary War.

Following him were about a thousand men, many of whom had fought the British. An equal number of men in the state militia were called to put down the rebellion under the command of Major General William Shepard at the federal arsenal at Springfield. Shays's tattered troup—it could hardly be called an army—moved toward the arsenal and its supply of new rifles. When they came within range, Shepard ordered a volley of rifle fire into the advancing mob. Several of the rebels fell dead, and the others fled.

The uprising was over, but its impact remained. Throughout the thirteen former colonies, many people sympathized with the farmers who had been made reckless by the depressed economic conditions. Washington and other leaders worried that the country that had won the recent war would not be able to govern itself in peacetime. To those who held public office, Shays's Rebellion was a reminder that, unless a sound government could be established, the result might be anarchy.

In that year of ferment, the Annapolis recommendation implying a desire to strengthen the Union came before the

Continental Congress. On February 27, 1787, it passed the following resolution:

> That in the opinion of Congress, it is expedient that on the second Monday in May next, a Convention of delegates, who shall have been appointed by the several states, be held in Philadelphia for the sole purpose of revising the Articles of Confederation, and reporting to Congress and the several legislatures, such alterations and provisions as shall, when agreed to in Congress, and confirmed by the states, render the Federal Constitution adequate to the exigencies of Government, and the Preservation of the Union.

One by one, all of the thirteen states—except Rhode Island—responded by electing delegates to Philadelphia. In Providence, state officeholders were afraid that a new strong central government would replace their paper money with coin, which they opposed. And so the state, which bore the formal name of Rhode Island and the Providence Plantations, was absent.

One of the first delegates to arrive in Philadelphia was James Madison. Eleven days before the appointed date, he rode by horseback from New York, where he was a member of the Continental Congress, to be fully prepared for what he had been working for years to achieve. In his methodical way, he had set down a four-stage procedure. By merely being present in Philadelphia, the delegates would accomplish his first goal. The second step was to agree and sign a new document. Third, the document would be submitted to Congress, and fourth, the states would hold separate ratification conventions.

His state of Virginia sent an outstanding group of men to Philadelphia. In addition to himself and Washington, it in-

cluded Governor Edmund Randolph, as well as Judge John
Blair, George Mason, and George Wythe, all distinguished
lawyers. Patrick Henry, the fiery orator of "give me liberty
or give me death" fame, had been elected a delegate but had
declined to serve because he was suspicious of any moves to
diminish the powers of the state. Another eminent Virgin-
ian, Thomas Jefferson—the author of the Declaration of Independence—was not there, and yet he was a strong
supporter of the convention's aims. In Paris as the American
minister to France, he kept in touch with developments by
correspondence with Madison.

Also absent was John Adams of Massachusetts, who was in
London as the American minister to England. Like Jefferson, he kept in touch with the convention by mail, but his
influence was felt even at the long distance from London.
Frequently during the convention, the *Philadelphia Gazette*
advertised a new book he had written, setting forth his governmental ideas, which presumably was read by many of the
delegates.

Two or three days before the convention officially opened,
the Virginia delegation met to agree on a common proposal.
As the prime movers in calling the convention, the Virgin-
ians felt it would be wise to have a specific plan ready for
consideration. They proceeded to draft such a plan to be
presented as soon as a sufficient number of delegates arrived
to make a quorum.

Altogether, seventy-four delegates were elected to the
convention, but only fifty-five attended. Yet there were
never more than thirty delegates present at any session, because many came and then left to look after their own business. Who were these delegates?

Thirty-three were lawyers. About half of them were college graduates—nine from the College of New Jersey, later renamed Princeton; five from William and Mary; four from Yale; three from Harvard; two from Columbia; and one from Pennsylvania. Almost all were well-to-do men who believed that the protection of property was a prime function of government. Eleven were involved in manufacturing, shipping, or similar businesses. Fourteen had invested money in land speculation in the West. Sixteen owned slaves. Only a handful were of humble origin or modest means. In an era when the major occupation of most Americans was farming, thirteen owned large farms or plantations while only two owned small farms. Not one delegate represented the working people.

One of the most striking things about this group of men was the wealth of political experience that they had. Thirty-three had served as representatives in the Continental Congress. Eight had signed the Declaration of Independence— Elbridge Gerry, Roger Sherman, Benjamin Franklin, Robert Morris, George Clymer, James Wilson, George Read, and George Wythe. All but two or three of them had served as public officials of their colony or state. Twenty had helped write the constitutions of their states.

Perhaps they were not "an assembly of demi-gods," as Jefferson described them, but they certainly were a distinguished body. One French observer at the convention wrote that it was composed of "the most enlightened men of the continent." Not only that, most of the delegates knew one another—from school or military service or politics. That made their meetings, discussions, and negotiations easier.

On the morning of May 14, the date set for its first meeting, the convention finally assembled and its official minutes recorded the following:

On Monday, the 14th day of May A.D. 1787, and in the eleventh year of the independence of the United States of America, at the State House in the City of Philadelphia, in virtue of appointments from their respective states, sundry delegates to the Federal Convention appeared; but a majority of the states not being represented, the members present adjourned, from day to day until Friday, the 25th of said month.

Day by day, Washington and the other delegates from Virginia and Pennsylvania went to the convention hall, waiting for enough other delegates to arrive to make a quorum. Madison was not concerned. The weather was rainy and the roads poor.

On May 17, the South Carolina delegates appeared. The following day, the New Yorkers showed up. On May 21, some delegates from Delaware arrived, followed the next day by the representatives of North Carolina. At last, on Friday May 25, eleven days after the convention had been due to open, New Jersey appeared, becoming the seventh state on hand and establishing a quorum for the convention.

Very likely, it was during one of those waiting days that Washington spoke the famous words that would be attributed to him by one of his fellow delegates years afterward:

It is too probable that no plan we propose will be adopted. Perhaps another dreadful conflict is to be sustained. If to please the people, we offer what we ourselves disapprove, how can we afterward defend our work? Let us raise a standard to which the wise and the honest can repair. The event is in the hand of God.

During the same period of suspense, another delegate from Virginia—George Mason—wrote to his son:

The Eyes of the United States are turned upon this Assembly and their Expectations raised to a very high Degree. May God grant that we may be able to gratify them by establishing a wise and just government.

2

The Delegates Meet

IT WAS RAINING on the morning of Friday May 25, when the delegates arrived on foot, on horse, and by carriage at the doors of the red brick building then known as the Pennsylvania State House. On their right as they entered was the large room in which the state court sat. On their left was the room used by the Pennsylvania legislature when it was in session—a historic chamber, even then. It was there, in 1775, that the Continental Congress had appointed Washington to command the Continental Army. It was there, in 1776, that the Declaration of Independence had been signed.

A spacious room, it measured a full forty feet in length and also in width, with a white plaster ceiling twenty feet above the floor. A wooden railing with a gate in the center split the room from east to west. The walls were painted gray, broken by high windows that had been shut for privacy and to prevent flies from swarming in. As a result, the delegates were plagued by heat instead. They sat at small tables, each covered with a green baize cloth and having a silver inkwell along with a supply of quill pens.

Outside, freshly spread sand covered cobblestoned Chestnut Street to muffle the sound of horses' hooves and passing carts so that the delegates' deliberations would not be disturbed. Guards stood at the State House entrance to keep the curious at a distance. The delegates felt that only in secrecy could they speak frankly and perhaps change their minds without embarrassment.

As soon as the delegates were seated that morning—there were twenty-nine present—they proceeded to the election of a president. Robert Morris nominated Washington, which everybody had expected and desired. Elected unanimously, he took his place in the president's chair on a low platform on the east side of the chamber. At the top of the chair's high back was carved what could be considered either a rising or a setting sun.

Today, we know the details of what happened at that first session and subsequent meetings mainly because of James Madison. Although some others took brief notes, Madison himself assumed the task, without objection from anyone, of recording everything that happened. He afterward explained how he did it:

I chose a seat in front of the presiding member, with the other members on my right and left hand. In this favorable position for hearing all that passed, I noted . . . in abbreviation and marks intelligible to myself what was read from the chair or spoken by the members; and losing not a moment unnecessarily beyond the adjournment and reassembling of the convention, I was enabled to write out my daily notes. . . . I was not absent a single day, nor more than a casual fraction of an hour in any day; so that I could not have lost a single speech, unless a very short one.

On Monday May 28, Franklin made his first appearance at the convention in a most unusual way. Suffering from gout, he could not get around easily, and to solve his transportation problem, he had imported a sedan chair from Paris. It was one of the sights of Philadelphia, an enclosed chair with glass windows, carried on poles twelve feet long by four husky prisoners from the Walnut Street jail.

Carefully, they carried the chair—with Franklin inside it—from his home to the State House, then up five steps at the entrance, and into the legislative chamber. Franklin was helped out of the chair to an armchair at the table reserved for the Pennsylvania delegation. But that day the convention did no more than consider the rules for its proceedings.

On Tuesday, Madison noted in his journal, "Mr. Randolph then opened the main business."

Mr. Randolph was Edmund Randolph, whose rapid political rise had started with his election as Virginia's attorney general at the age of just twenty-three. Now thirty-four, he had recently been chosen governor of his state. While he did have a keen mind, he owed his advancement at least partly to his being a notably handsome member of a leading Virginia family.

Speaking for nearly three hours, Randolph outlined the familiar defects of the Articles of Confederation and called for a strong central government. He then presented Virginia's plan—a group of fifteen "resolves" that had been prepared by the state's delegates as a basis for the deliberations of the convention.

The next day the convention formed itself into a committee of the whole, a parliamentary device used by legislatures so that its members could speak informally. After Nathaniel Gorham of Massachusetts was elected chairman, he took his place on the dais as Washington stepped down to sit with the Virginia delegation.

Immediately, Randolph moved that the delegates should commit themselves to the proposition "that a national government ought to be established consisting of a supreme Legislative, Executive, and Judiciary." Complete silence fell in the hall as the delegates realized the meaning of that simple, far-reaching sentence. It called for more than just an expansion of the existing Articles of Confederation—it was creating a new kind of national government.

Wythe of Virginia spoke up. "From the silence of the house," he said, "I presume the gentlemen are prepared to pass on the resolution."

But Pierce Butler of South Carolina arose. "The house is not so prepared," he said. And then debate erupted.

This first debate indicated clearly that the delegates were practical men, concerned about finding solutions to the real problems facing them. Madison, for instance, was tireless as both a recorder and participant in the discussions. Washington, although he did not utter a word on the convention floor, still was a powerful force for unity by his mere presence and by his words during informal gatherings after each session ended. Several others played leading roles throughout the convention. James Wilson of Philadelphia, a studious lawyer wearing steel-rimmed spectacles, right from the outset was one of the most convincing advocates of a strong— and democratic—system for governing the United States. Born in Scotland, where he had attended two universities, he still spoke with the burr of Edinburgh. What he kept saying about how the new government should be organized made him the unsung hero of the Constitutional Convention.

Scholarly James Wilson, the unsung hero of the Constitutional Convention. *Courtesy American Philosophical Society*

Wilson's major contribution would be nearly forgotten because of a personal failing that ruined his reputation a few years later. He had invested in huge tracts of Western land with borrowed money, gambling on making a fortune. Instead, he was so pressed by the people he owed that in the

1790s he broke down and died in disgrace. Yet this man would be included among the "deepest thinkers and most exact reasoners" in Philadelphia in 1787 by the outstanding British authority Lord Bryce when he wrote his masterly essay on American democracy a century afterward.

Roger Sherman of Connecticut, at the age of sixty-six, was Wilson's senior by more than twenty years and could hardly have been more reliable, both personally and politically. A lean, tall, plainly dressed man, he was one of the handful of delegates with a working class background. As a shoemaker, lacking any formal education, he had still managed to study law. Showing exceptional ability at smoothing over disputes, he rose to be a judge and then was elected to the Continental Congress. There, Thomas Jefferson pointed him out to a visitor one day, saying, "That is Mr. Sherman of Connecticut, who never said a foolish thing in his life."

But the body of delegates in Philadelphia also included some lesser figures who did a lot of talking without saying much—and Elbridge Gerry of Massachusetts provided a prime example. A small, worried-looking man with a large nose, he kept jumping up to speak at length. Yet his opinions veered back and forth like a pendulum. Was he for a strong national government? Or did he care more about states' rights? Nobody could be sure.

The convention's first debate, over Randolph's proposal for a new national government, actually went quite swiftly. After only a few days of discussion, the group agreed to vote on the issue. Six states—Massachusetts, Pennsylvania, Delaware, Virginia, North Carolina, and South Carolina—voted in favor. Connecticut voted against the proposal. New York was divided. New Jersey did not have a quorum and so did not vote.

This meant that, by the narrowest of margins and just for

Roger Sherman of Connecticut, the former shoemaker who played an important role at the Constitutional Convention. *Courtesy Independence National Historical Park*

the time being, the Virginia plan had won its first important test. According to the rules the convention had adopted, any proposal the delegates agreed to was subject to later reconsideration. However, the victory for Randolph's initial motion definitely strengthened the forces favoring a new federal system.

The convention then went on to the next Randolph motion, regarding the proposed new national legislature. With no serious dissent, the delegates agreed that it should consist of two branches, unlike the Continental Congress, which had only one. An anecdote explains why the group favored two branches. When Jefferson, returning from France, asked Washington why he had agreed to a second chamber, Washington in turn asked him, "Why do you pour your coffee into your saucer?" "To cool it," Jefferson replied. "Even so," said Washington, "we pour legislation into the senatorial saucer to cool it."

The next question raised at the convention revealed a serious division among the delegates. It was on a crucial aspect of the Virginia plan: "that the members of the first branch of the national legislature should be elected by the people of the several states." That, too, was different from the Continental Congress, whose members were elected by state legislatures.

In the debate that followed, the most vigorous supporters of a strong national government—men like Madison, Wilson, and Gouverneur Morris of Pennsylvania—favored election by the people. Opposed were Sherman and Gerry among others, holding that the representatives should continue to be chosen by state legislatures.

"The people should have as little to do as may be about the government," said Sherman. "They want information and are constantly liable to be misled." "They are dupes of pretended patriots," said Gerry, whose home state of Massachusetts had just suppressed Shays's Rebellion.

Mason of Virginia replied, "The larger branch is to be the grand depository of the democratic principle of government." Wilson added, "Without the confidence of the people, no government, least of all a republican government, can long subsist." Madison insisted that election by the people was indispensable to any plan of government. Their views prevailed, by a vote of six states to two, with two states abstaining.

From consideration of the new national legislature, the convention moved on to the subject of the executive branch. The question was posed by the Virginia resolve: "A national executive, chosen by the national legislature and ineligible a second time, ought to enjoy the executive rights vested in Congress by the confederation, and a general authority to execute the national laws."

Wilson, taking one of the most significant steps of the entire convention, moved that the executive branch consist of one person. There was a stunned silence in the room. The delegates all remembered their war for independence from the despotic King George III of England. To many of them, a single executive would be the equivalent of a king—and kings led to tyranny.

Benjamin Franklin broke the silence. The question was of great importance, he said, and he wished the gentlemen would deliver their sentiments on it.

John Rutledge of South Carolina arose. He said he favored a single executive but was against giving him the power of war and peace. Sherman said he viewed the executive as an agent and servant of the legislature, which should have the power to appoint one or more. Randolph said he strongly opposed a single executive, seeing in it "the fetus of monarchy."

The question was so touchy that the delegates decided to consider executive powers and term of office before deciding the matter of size. They easily agreed on the powers—"to carry into effect the national laws and to appoint to offices in cases not otherwise provided for." But they had trouble in deciding how the executive was to be chosen and how long the term of office would be.

Three years, said Wilson and Sherman. No, seven years without any possibility of reelection, said Mason. Gunning Bedford of Delaware protested against so long a term. What if the electors chose an incompetent executive? How would they remove him or them?

Five states voted for a seven-year-term, four states against. Later, of course, the convention agreed to a four-year term, with no mention of a ban on reelection.

How would the executive be chosen? By the people, said Wilson. But Sherman dissented. "I am for its appointment by the national legislature, and for making it absolutely dependent on that body, whose will it is to execute," he said. The delegates at that time agreed with Sherman, although they later reversed themselves.

But the major question remained: should the executive be one person or three? Mason strongly opposed a one-man executive. He could never agree, he said, to give all the rights of the people to one man, which he thought would inevitably lead to a king, perhaps a hereditary monarchy. Randolph also was for a multiple executive, one from each of the three geographical areas of the country.

The solemn, bespectacled Wilson carried the burden of those who believed in a single executive. He pointed out that all of the states had one man at the helm. Moreover, he argued, "if there should be three heads to the national executive, there could be neither vigor nor tranquillity."

When the vote was taken, seven states voted in favor of a single executive. Only three states—New York, Delaware, and Maryland—opposed it. The reason for the favorable vote, historians generally have agreed, was that the delegates felt that George Washington was the obvious choice for a single executive, and they had faith in him and his democratic principles.

After voting to establish a national judiciary, the committee of the whole returned to one of the most vexing problems before it. Again, they debated about how members of the legislature would be elected. A week before they had voted for election by the people. But the small states were not satisfied. In the Continental Congress each state, no matter how large or small, had one vote. Under the new proposal, the small states obviously would lose some of their power.

The immediate question was how to elect members of the second branch of the legislature. John Dickinson of Delaware moved that they be elected by state legislatures, giving two reasons—that this would tie state governments to the national legislature and would create a chamber composed of more distinguished citizens than those who had to face popular elections.

"Let our government be like that of the solar system," Dickinson said. "Let the general government be like the sun and the states be the planets, repelled yet attracted, and the whole moving regularly and harmoniously in their several orbits."

The delegates accepted this analogy. There was little opposition to the idea of electing members of the second branch by the state legislature as a concession to those delegates who believed firmly in states' rights. For the moment, the delegates avoided the basic question of how many members the body would have. It was an issue of paramount importance for the small states. They would never, they said, give up their rights to equal representation in the legislature with the larger states, no matter what the population differences were.

On Monday June 11, plain old Roger Sherman, the former shoemaker from Connecticut, made a proposal that was voted down but would eventually save the convention from failure. In the words of Madison: "Mr. Sherman proposed that the portion of suffrage in the first branch should be according to the respective numbers of free inhabitants, and that in the second branch, or Senate, each state should have one vote and no more."

Two days later, on June 13, the committee of the whole completed its work on the Virginia resolves and reported to the full convention. The fifteen Virginia resolves had grown to nineteen. Together, they contained the outline of a new government. But the delegates from the small states still were not satisfied.

The task of leading the argument for the small states fell to William Paterson of New Jersey, a forty-two-year-old former attorney general of the state, a skilled lawyer and advocate. Protesting against throwing the states into what he called a "hotchpot," he presented a plan that did what his state's instructions called for—nothing more than revising the Articles of Confederation.

The New Jersey plan preserved a congress with equal votes in a one-house legislature. It granted to the United States revenues from duties, stamps, and a post office, but no other funds except by requisition from the states. It established an executive consisting of several persons, and it conferred on state courts original jurisdiction over infractions of United States laws.

The two plans clearly displayed opposite views. The Virginia plan called for a truly national government, the New Jersey plan merely for a stronger confederation of states, with all of them equal in power.

Paterson defended his plan. "The confederation is in the nature of a compact," he said, "and can any state, unless by the consent of the whole, either in policy or law, withdraw its powers?" He added that while the largest states would contribute the most, they had more to protect. "A rich state and a poor state are in the same relation as a rich individual and a poor one," he declared. "The liberty for the latter must be preserved."

In reply, Wilson said he could not persuade himself that a national government was bad. "Why should a national government be unpopular?" he demanded. "Has it less dignity? Will each citizen enjoy under it less liberty or protection? Will a citizen of Delaware be degraded by becoming a citizen of the United States?"

The Virginia plan or the New Jersey plan? The delegates had to choose.

Seven states voted for the Virginia plan—Massachusetts, Connecticut, Pennsylvania, Virginia, North Carolina, South Carolina, and Georgia. Three states—New York, New Jersey, and Delaware—opposed it, and Maryland remained undecided.

But the Virginia plan was only a road map, not a detailed chart for organizing a government. There were many gaps to be filled in. The delegates proceeded to discuss them one by one, conducting what has since been called "the great debate" of the Constitutional Convention. Day after day, the delegates worked on the Virginia plan, word by word, clause by clause, with the small states fighting to preserve their rights.

There was agreement on two important points—a two-year term for representatives in the first branch of the legislature and a term of six years in the second branch. It was also agreed that senators be not less than thirty years of age and that they be selected by the state legislatures.

Still, the delegates seemed hopelessly split on how the states should be represented in both branches of the legislature. The large states were for proportional representation, based on population, which would give them the power they said they deserved, but the small states were adamant for the same equal representation they had under the Articles of Confederation.

From his seat in the rear of the room, the venerable Franklin spoke up. "The diversity of opinions turns on two points," he said. "If a proportional representation takes place, the small states contend that their liberties will be in danger. If an equality of votes is to be put in its place, large states say their money will be in danger." He paused and then offered one of his most famous sayings. "When a broad table is to be made and the edges of a plank do not fit," Ben Franklin told his fellow delegates, "the artist takes a little from both and makes a good joint. In like manner, both sides must part with some of their demands, in order that they both join in some accommodating proposition."

Franklin then suggested that the states have an equal number of senators, just as Sherman had proposed earlier. But the time was not yet ripe for compromise. A motion for equality in the Senate resulted in a tie, five states for it and five states against, with Georgia divided.

The convention had reached an impasse. It appointed a committee to see if some compromise could be worked out over the July 4 weekend. After the holiday, the committee made its report. It recommended:

1. That, in the first branch of the legislature, there should be one representative for each 40,000 inhabitants;

2. That the first branch should have the power to originate all bills for raising and appropriating money;

3. That, in the second branch, each state should have an equal vote.

Even though they objected to some of the compromise, Gerry and Mason urged acceptance. But the three leaders favoring a strong central government—Madison, Wilson, and Gouverneur Morris—were not convinced that the small states should have an equal role in the second branch.

The split was so great and the arguments so hot that Washington on July 10 wrote to Hamilton, who had departed for New York, that "I almost despair of seeing a favorable issue to the proceedings of our convention, and do therefore repent of having had any agency in the business."

That despair was shared by many of the delegates when they met again on July 16. That day, the final vote on the Connecticut compromise originally proposed by Roger Sherman was taken. Five states voted for it—Connecticut, New Jersey, Delaware, Maryland, and North Carolina. Four states voted against—Virginia, South Carolina, Pennsylvania, and Georgia. Massachusetts was split and New York absent.

Randolph, the original sponsor of the Virginia plan, felt disheartened at the close vote against his proposal. Paterson, who had proposed the New Jersey plan, suggested an adjournment, which would mean, in effect, ending the convention. Luther Martin of Maryland said later, "We were on the verge of dissolution, scarce held together by a hair."

But both sides were equally concerned about the necessity for working together. The next morning, before the formal convention convened, representatives of the larger states got together in an informal meeting. Should they try to overturn the vote of the day before?

All of them knew, though, that if the three nonvoting states—New York, New Hampshire, and Rhode Island—could vote, they would support the smaller states. In reality, there were eight states in favor of what came to be called "the great compromise."

So the large states accepted their defeat. They knew that even if they could unite and override the vote of the day before, that would mean a walkout by the small states and the end of the convention. Therefore, they accepted the compromise as final. Had they decided othewise, most historians agree, the convention would have failed.

With acceptance of the compromise, though, delegates from the small states regained their good cheer and the convention moved rapidly forward. The delegates quickly disposed of some of the remaining issues. They voted to make all laws and treaties of the United States the supreme law of the land, to give a veto power to the executive, and to give two seats in the second branch of the legislature to each state.

In ten weeks of concentrated effort, the preliminary work of the convention was done. The delegates had faced most of the major issues in writing a new constitution and had resolved many. Now it was the time to have what they had arrived at put into a coherent written form. By the rules of the convention, they would still be able then to reconsider anything they had already voted on—and there still remained a few important issues unresolved.

The convention appointed a committee of five to bring back a written constitution based on the many resolutions they had passed. The members of the committee were nicely balanced geographically: two from the South, Rutledge of

South Carolina and Randolph of Virginia; two from the North, Gorham of Massachusetts and Oliver Ellsworth of Connecticut; and one from the middle states, Wilson of Pennsylvania.

With that, the other delegates went on a ten-day holiday.

3

A Second Great Compromise

As THE MIDSUMMER HEAT made Philadelphia humid and uncomfortable, most of the delegates scattered for a brief vacation. Washington traveled with Gouverneur Morris back to Valley Forge where he inspected the camp, now in ruins, at which he and the American army had spent the snowy winter of 1777. He also fished for trout there.

On August 6, Washington, now well rested, returned to preside over the convention. That day John Rutledge of South Carolina, the chairman of the committee on detail, reported its draft of a constitution—seven pages long, with broad margins for notes to be made by delegates. Using the Virginia plan as its base, the new constitution also included some features of the New Jersey plan. The document, largely the work of Rutledge and Wilson, consisted of a preamble and twenty-three articles divided into forty-one separate sections. By the rules of the convention, any of these sections could be reopened, reargued, and voted upon again.

For the first time, the document called the national legislature "Congress." The "first branch" became the "House of Representatives" and the "second branch" the "Senate." The "Supreme Tribunal" of the judiciary became the "Supreme Court" and the "executive branch" the "President of the United States." All of these changes were accepted without argument during the next five weeks as the delegates took up the committee report, section by section, making many basic decisions.

They declined to set up ownership of property as a condition of voting, leaving voter qualifications to the states.

They agreed on the powers of Congress, changing words to clarify some of the details. For example, "to make war" was changed "to declare war" and "to raise armies" became "to raise and support armies."

They rejected a proposal that members of Congress should be paid by their states.

They confirmed the power of the President to veto a bill passed by Congress and the power of Congress to repass the bill over his veto by a two-thirds majority in each chamber.

They gave Congress the power to levy and collect taxes, which it did not have under the Articles of Confederation.

They decided to fix the seat of the new national government in a federal district that would be ten miles square.

They expanded the powers of the President to include making a report to Congress on the State of the Union, recommending legislation to Congress, receiving ambassadors, and granting pardons.

They also rejected a proposed Bill of Rights as unnecessary.

In contrast to the long and detailed debates about the

powers of Congress and of the President, there was surprisingly little discussion about the judiciary system. The delegates agreed to establish a Supreme Court and inferior courts to be set up by Congress. They gave the federal courts the power to decide on cases arising under United States laws and the Constitution, which was declared to be "the supreme law" of the land. They also gave the Supreme Court jurisdiction over cases affecting ambassadors and between states, and specified that the court could hear appeals from lower courts in other cases.

Nowhere in the Constitution or in the discussions about the judiciary did the delegates give the Supreme Court the specific power to declare laws unconstitutional. That power, which would later be described as "implied" by the Constitution, would be assumed by the Supreme Court itself.

At the convention, the delegates remained split on a method of electing the President and so deferred action by referring the matter to a committee. Then they turned their attention to another major issue that divided them, the regulation of commerce. It was the refusal of the states to grant such powers to the Continental Congress under the Articles of Confederation that had produced the chaos in commerce that was one of the main reasons the convention had been called.

When the delegates considered a clause giving Congress the power to pass navigation acts, there was a notable split based on differing economic interests. The Northern states, which had a strong shipping trade, favored legislation that would take effect on gaining just a majority vote. The Southern states, having little shipping and fearing unfair treatment by the North, favored a two-thirds vote, which would make their voice more powerful.

Behind that mercantile disagreement lay the explosive

question of slavery, although the word was not mentioned in the proposed constitutional clause. But the issue was there, and every delegate knew it.

The committee on detail had recommended a prohibition on taxing "the migration or importation of such persons as the several states think proper to admit" and had added "nor shall such migration or importation be prohibited." Translated, that meant approval of a continuation of the slave trade from Africa to the United States.

When the convention began deliberating about this clause, Luther Martin of Maryland brought the slavery issue directly in front of the delegates. He made a motion to give Congress the power to tax or forbid the importation of slaves, the direct opposite of what the committee had proposed. He argued that a provision already accepted tentatively, whereby three-fifths of the slave population in the South would be counted to determine its representation in Congress, would encourage the slave trade. Therefore, he declared, it was unreasonable that the slave traffic should be free of taxation.

The question before the convention was not whether slavery should be prohibited, but who should control it—the states or the national government? Sherman of Connecticut said he opposed the slave trade, but thought it was a state not a national problem. Rutledge of South Carolina put the Southern position openly, holding that a tax or prohibition of the slave trade would hurt the vital economic interests of the South.

"The true question is whether the Southern states shall or shall not be parties to the Union," he said. "If the Northern states consult their own interest, they will not oppose the increase of slaves, which will increase the commodities of which they will become the carriers." It was a clear reference to the fact that Northern shipping carried slaves from Africa to the United States.

The most powerful attack on slavery came from a Southerner. George Mason of Virginia, one of the most respected men in all the states, had been the author of the Virginia Declaration of Rights. Although he himself owned 200 slaves, he opposed the whole institution.

"The infernal traffic," he said, was a national and a moral issue. Not only did slavery discourage arts and manufactures, he said, but it also produced "the most pernicious effect on manners." He went on: "Every master of slaves is born a petty tyrant. They bring the judgment of Heaven upon a country." It was essential, he declared, that the new government prevent any increase in slavery.

To this, Charles Pinckney of South Carolina replied that slavery was justified by the example of ancient Rome and Greece. If the Southern states were left alone, he continued, they probably would stop the slave trade themselves, relying on the natural increase of the slave population to provide an adequate labor force. But his cousin and colleague, Charles Cotesworth Pinckney, concentrated on the fundamental point that South Carolina and Georgia could not do without slaves. To end the slave trade would mean excluding them from the Union, he warned.

Gouverneur Morris, who had spoken against slavery and the slave trade, tried to find a middle ground. On his motion, a committee of one from each state was appointed to solve the impasse. It came back in a few days with the second great compromise of the convention. Without it, Hamilton would later say, "no union could possibly have been formed."

By its terms, the Southern states agreed that Congress would have the power to prohibit the importation of slaves after the year 1808. They also accepted a simple majority vote on navigation laws, which went against their own economic interests. In return, the Northern states agreed that the import duty on slaves would not be more than ten dollars a head and that slaves would be counted, for the purposes of representation and taxes, in the ratio of five slaves to three free white persons.

With that compromise, the convention moved swiftly to complete its work. The delegates voted to allow the admission of new states, which would then have the same rights as the original thirteen. They approved a method of amending the Constitution, if need be. They also decided that the new Constitution would be submitted for adoption to a convention of delegates in each state, not to the state legislatures. And, more important, instead of requiring a unanimous vote for approval, it would go into effect when approved by nine states.

Then the convention was ready for the report of its special committee on how to elect the President. Judge David Brearley of New Jersey, the committee chairman, read its recommendations fixing the term of office of the President at four years instead of the seven years previously proposed, with no mention of whether he would be eligible for reelection, which meant that he would be. In addition, the committee proposed that he be chosen by electors elected by the people. And, for the first time, a new post was mentioned, that of Vice President, the person who came in second in the selection by the electors.

But what if the electors could not agree? Sherman offered a solution—that the election would then fall to the House of Representatives, with each state casting one vote. The committee's report was approved.

Now it was the turn of another committee to put the Con-

Gouverneur Morris, who was largely responsible for the wording of the final draft of the Constitution. *Courtesy American Philosophical Society*

stitution into its final form. The convention appointed five of its ablest members to serve on this group, with William Samuel Johnson, the new president of Columbia College in New York, as its chairman. Besides Madison and Hamilton, the committee included Rufus King of Massachusetts and

Gouverneur Morris of Pennsylvania, who received the assignment of actually writing the new document.

A warm, likeable man, Morris had spoken more often than any other delegate on the floor of the convention. One historian counted the number of times at 173—compared with Wilson's 161, Sherman's 138, Mason's 136, and Gerry's 119. But Morris's contributions were not only in speaking often. He brought zest and often wit to a weary group of delegates.

Only thirty-five years old, Morris had already made a name for himself. He had been a treasurer of the Continental Congress during the Revolution and had become a friend of Washington. A bachelor, he was known as a ladies' man, always looking for a new conquest. He made a picturesque appearance, walking with the aid of a wooden leg made of oak with a knob at its end. He had not lost his leg jumping from a woman's balcony, as some gossips said, but had so severely damaged it while trying to stop a pair of runaway horses that it had to be amputated.

We know from two sources that Morris wrote the Constitution. Long afterward, he himself mentioned in a letter to a friend that the document had been "written by the fingers that wrote this letter." And Madison, looking back in 1831, set down the words: "The finish given to the style and arrangement of the Constitution fairly belongs to the pen of Mr. Morris." Of course, the other members of the committee were consulted and had to concur on the final words, which they did. In addition, Morris probably consulted with his colleague from Pennsylvania, the scholarly James Wilson, who was not a member of the committee.

Morris had the knack of simplifying complex language. He compressed the twenty-three articles that had been reported by the committee on detail a month earlier into seven. The wording was not merely condensed, but also clarified and polished. But his great contribution was in revising the preamble. What he accomplished is clearly shown by comparing one passage before and after he took up his pen:

As Proposed	*As Rewritten*
We the people of the States of New Hampshire, Massachusetts, Rhode Island and the Providence Plantations, Connecticut, New Jersey, Pennsylvania, Delaware, Maryland, Virginia, North Carolina, South Carolina and Georgia, do ordain, declare and establish the following Constitution for the government of ourselves and our Posterity.	We the people of the United States, in Order to form a more perfect Union, establish Justice, insure domestic Tranquility, provide for the common defence, promote the general Welfare, and secure the Blessings of Liberty to ourselves and our Posterity, do ordain and establish this Constitution for the United States of America.

"The seven verbs rolled out—to form, establish, insure, provide, promote, secure, ordain," the writer Catherine Drinker Bowen marveled in her *Miracle at Philadelphia*. "One might challenge the centuries to better these verbs."

But the change was made not only for its literary superiority. It was a practical matter, too. The earlier version had been written under the assumption that all the states would have to accept the Constitution before it could be adopted. Now, though, since only nine states would have to ratify it, there was no reason to list the whole roster; indeed, it might cause confusion, should any state refuse to ratify.

The new Constitution was reported back to the full convention on September 12. There is no record of any objection to the new preamble. Washington later said that the

W E the People of the States of New-Hampſhire, Maſſachuſetts, Rhode-Iſland and Providence Plan-tations, Connecticut, New-York, New-Jerſey, Penn-ſylvania, Delaware, Maryland, Virginia, North-Caro-lina, South-Carolina, and Georgia, do ordain, declare and eſtabliſh the following Conſtitution for the Govern-ment of Ourſelves and our Poſterity.

ARTICLE I.
The ſtile of this Government ſhall be, " The United States of America."

II.
The Government ſhall conſiſt of ſupreme legiſlative, executive and judicial powers.

III.
The legiſlative power ſhall be veſted in a Congreſs, to conſiſt of two ſeparate and diſtinct bodies of men, a Houſe of Repreſentatives, and a Senate; ~~each of which ſhall, in all caſes, have a negative on the other. The Legiſlature ſhall meet on the firſt Monday in December in every year.~~

[margin annotation:] ✻ The Legislature ſhall meet at leaſt once in every year and that meeting ſhall be on the firſt Monday in December unleſs a different day ſhall be appointed by Law.

IV.
Sect. 1. The Members of the Houſe of Repreſentatives ſhall be choſen eve-ry ſecond year, by the people of the ſeveral States comprehended within this Union. The qualifications of the electors ſhall be the ſame, from time to time, as thoſe of the electors in the ſeveral States, of the moſt numerous branch of their own legiſlatures.

Sect. 2. Every Member of the Houſe of Repreſentatives ſhall be of the age of twenty-five years at leaſt; ſhall have been a citizen ▓ the United States for at leaſt ▓▓▓ years before his election; and ſhall be, at the time of his e-lection, ▓▓▓▓▓ of the State in which he ſhall be choſen.

Sect. 3. The Houſe of Repreſentatives ſhall, at its firſt formation, and until the number of citizens and inhabitants ſhall be taken in the manner herein af-ter deſcribed, conſiſt of ſixty-five Members, of whom three ſhall be choſen in New-Hampſhire, eight in Maſſachuſetts, one in Rhode-Iſland and Providence Plantations, five in Connecticut, ſix in New-York, four in New-Jerſey. eight in Pennſylvania, one in Delaware, ſix in Maryland, ten in Virginia, five in North-Carolina, five in South-Carolina, and three in Georgia.

Sect. 4. As the proportions of numbers in the different States will alter from time to time; as ſome of the States may hereafter be divided; as others may be enlarged by addition of territory; as two or more States may be united; as new States will be erected within the limits of the United States, the Legiſla-ture ſhall, in each of theſe caſes, regulate the number of repreſentatives by the number of inhabitants, according to the ▓▓▓▓▓▓▓▓ the rate of one for every forty thouſand. *Provided that every State ſhall have at leaſt one repreſentative.*

Sect. 5. All bills for raiſing or appropriating money, and for fixing the ſala-ries of the officers of government, ſhall originate in the Houſe of Repreſenta-tives, and ſhall not be altered or amended by the Senate. No money ſhall be drawn from the public Treaſury, but in purſuance of appropriations that ſhall originate in the Houſe of Repreſentatives.

[margin:] ... the ... ſecond ... ſtruck out

Sect. 6. The Houſe of Repreſentatives ſhall have the ſole power of impeach-ment. It ſhall chooſe its Speaker and other officers.

Sect. 7. Vacancies in the Houſe of Repreſentatives ſhall be ſupplied by writs of election from the executive authority of the State, in the repreſentation from which they ſhall happen.   V.

One of the working copies of a preliminary version of the Con-stitution. *Courtesy National Archives* delegates on the whole were pleased when they saw "the propositions reduced to form and connected together."

By this time, however, the delegates were tired and impatient to complete their work and return home. Quickly, they approved the document, making only some minor word changes here and there. Yet in their haste they perpetrated what some people later said was their most serious mistake—they once again rejected a proposed Bill of Rights.

Mason of Virginia said the Constitution should have one, and he seconded a motion to include a Bill of Rights when Gerry of Massachusetts proposed it. Hamilton, Wilson, and Sherman, among others, opposed it as unnecessary. They looked upon the entire Constitution as a bill of rights in itself, with all its provisions protecting the people. Why, then, should there be a list of the things that Congress could not do after having specified what it could do? So the motion was defeated by a ten-to-nothing vote, with Massachusetts absent and New York not fully represented and so ineligible to vote.

Saturday September 15, the last working day of the convention, was marked by opposition to the new Constitution by three leading delegates—Randolph, Mason, and Gerry. Ironically, all of them had taken a major part in the discussions that had shaped it.

Randolph, the man who had presented the Virginia resolves that had given the convention its working base, now felt he must dissent from the final product. He said he was against the "indefinite and dangerous" powers given to Congress. Let the whole plan be turned over to the states to study, he suggested, let them propose amendments, and then let the result be considered at another general convention.

Mason of Virginia seconded the motion. He said he had

concluded that the new strong central government proposed would end in either a monarchy or a hereditary aristocracy. "This Constitution has been formed without the knowledge or idea of the people," he said. "A second convention will know more of the sense of the people."

The last speech of objection was made by Gerry, who had a long list of complaints. These related to excessive power for Congress, too long a term for Senators, the three-fifths slave count, and the duties of the Vice President. Wearied beyond patience by his whiny voice, the other delegates ignored his comments.

It was then six o'clock in the evening. The delegates had sat on this last working day since eleven that morning, without a recess for food or drink. They were ready to vote. Madison recorded the tally this way:

> On the question of the proposition of Mr. Randolph, all of the states answered no.
>
> On the question to agree to the [Constitution] as amended, all the states ay.
>
> The Constitution was then ordered to be engrossed.

Late that Saturday night, Jacob Shallus, assistant clerk of the Pennsylvania General Assembly, copied the final version of the Constitution on four large sheets of parchment. The following Monday morning, September 17, when the delegates assembled for their last day together, the secretary read it aloud to them.

When he finished, the ailing Franklin arose with a speech in one hand and asked his colleague Wilson to read it for him.

"Mr. President," Franklin had started, "I confess there are several parts of this Constitution which I cannot at present approve. But I am not sure I shall never approve them. For having lived so long, I have experienced many instances of being obliged by better information or fuller consideration to change opinions, even on important subjects, which I once thought to be right, but found to be otherwise. It is therefore that the older I grow, the more apt I am to doubt my own judgment and to pay more respect to the judgment of others."

Franklin went on to say that he was astonished to find that the Constitution approached as near perfection as it did. "And I think it will astonish our enemies, who are waiting with confidence to hear that our councils are confounded . . . and that our states are on the point of separation."

A practical man, Franklin offered a motion that the delegates sign the Constitution in this form: "Done in Convention by the Unanimous Consent of the States present the Seventeenth Day of September." Doing it that way would allow even dissenters to sign, for they would be avoiding a personal commitment.

In the chamber were six delegates who had attended most of the sessions but who had not said one word on the floor— William Blount of North Carolina, John Blair of Virginia, Nicholas Gilman of New Hampshire, Richard Bassett of Delaware, William Few of Georgia, and Jared Ingersoll of Pennsylvania. Blount broke his silence and said that he could not sign. Ingersoll arose and said he would sign. The other four still did not speak, but they did sign.

There was one more dramatic moment before the document was actually signed. Gorham of Massachusetts proposed a final change, that the number of citizens to be represented by each member of the House of Representatives be reduced from 40,000 to 30,000. Washington arose, seemingly for the purpose of putting the question to the delegates, but instead he made his first and only speech from the floor of the convention. Madison described what he said:

> Although his situation had hitherto restrained him from offering his sentiments on questions depending in the House, and it might be thought, ought now to impose silence on him, yet he could not forbear expressing his wish that the alteration proposed might take place. . . . Late as the present moment was for admitting amendments, he thought this of so much consequence that it would give much satisfaction to see it adopted.

No one argued. The change was made by unanimous vote.

The delegates also agreed to sign in the form suggested by Franklin, with ten states voting approval, one negative and one, South Carolina, divided.

Sometime in the late afternoon the signing began. Of forty-one delegates present on that historic occasion, thirty-eight signed. First came Washington, as president of the convention. Then, with Hamilton writing the name of each state on the document, its delegates came forward and signed. Only Randolph, Gerry, and Mason held back. When the turn of Delaware came, Read signed for himself and on behalf of Dickinson, who was absent because of illness. That made a total of thirty-nine signatures on the new Constitution.

While the last members were signing, Franklin looked at the president's chair with its painting of the sun and its rays. He remarked to some members sitting nearby that painters had often found it difficult to distinguish between a rising and setting sun. "I have," he said, "often and often in the course of the session, and the vicissitudes of my hopes and fears as to its issue, looked behind the President without

A detail from a painting of the signing of the Constitution on view at the Independence Hall National Historical Park. *Courtesy Independence National Historical Park*

being able at all to tell whether it was rising or setting. But now at length, I have the happiness to know that is a rising and not a setting sun."

In his usual brief and straightforward style, Washington recorded in his diary for that day that the Constitution had received the unanimous assent of eleven states and of Colonel Hamilton from New York, who was the only delegate from that state to be present.

"The business being thus closed," Washington wrote, "the members adjourned to the City Tavern, dined together and took a cordial leave of each other."

Now it was up to the people to consider the new Constitution—to accept or reject it.

4

Ratification

ON THE FOLLOWING MORNING William Jackson, the secretary of the convention, left Philadelphia by stagecoach. He was carrying the official copy of the new Constitution to be delivered to Congress in New York, then the nation's capital. He also took with him a resolution of the delegates, requesting Congress to submit the Constitution to conventions elected in each state for ratification, and a letter from Washington in his capacity as the president of the convention.

In his letter, Washington wrote about the Constitution:

That it will meet the full and entire approbation of every state is not perhaps to be expected; but each will doubtless consider, that had her interest alone been consulted, the consequences might have been particularly disagreeable or injurious to others; that it is liable to as few exceptions as could reasonably have been expected, we hope and believe; that it may promote lasting welfare of that country so dear to

51

A photograph of the first page of the Constitution on exhibit at the National Archives Building in Washington. *Courtesy National Archives*

us all, and secure her freedom and happiness, is our ardent
wish.

When Congress assembled on September 26, 1787, it was
by no means certain that the new Constitution would be accepted. Ranged against it were farmers who were concerned
about a distant government and state politicians fearful of
losing power. There was also widespread suspicion that a
central government would be insensitive to local issues, as
well as a concern among debtors that a new government and
a new sound money policy would cost them money. Further-
more, the American public was already noted for a general
revulsion against taxation. Underlying every other factor,
though, was a deep fear of change.

In favor of the new Constitution were most merchants,
lawyers, creditors, and those who believed that the Articles
of Confederation were not sufficient to govern a growing nation—indeed, that they had already failed. To them, as
Madison wrote, it was a simple question: "Whether the
Union shall or shall not be continued."

During the year-long struggle to ratify the Constitution,
two clearly defined sides emerged. Those in favor took the
name Federalists, and those opposed became Anti-Federalists. However, in many ways the names were deceiving.
Anti-Federalists actually believed in a federal system, with
the central government having little power and the states
more, while the Federalists supported a strong central government that had more power than the states. But the labels
stuck.

On both sides were patriotic citizens. Probably the most
compelling argument in favor of the Constitution was the
fact that George Washington approved of it. The support of
America's other great hero—the venerable Ben Franklin—

undoubtedly had an effect, too, even though his age made it unlikely that he would play any further public role. But younger men, especially Hamilton and Madison, also did much to influence their fellow Americans in the drive for ratification.

Leading figures in the fight against the Constitution included the doughty Patrick Henry of Virginia and Governor George Clinton of New York. Their cause received much assistance from three delegates who had left the convention in protest—Luther Martin of Maryland and John Lansing and Robert Yates of New York. Two men who had stayed on in Philadelphia—Mason of Virginia and the cranky Gerry of Massachusetts—also raised their voices condemning the product of the long summer's deliberations.

The first contest was in Congress, which had among its members ten of the delegates who had approved the Constitution in Philadelphia—John Langdon and Nicholas Gilman of New Hampshire, Nathaniel Gorham and Rufus King of Massachusetts, William Samuel Johnson of Connecticut, James Madison of Virginia, William Blount of North Carolina, Pierce Butler of South Carolina, and William Few and William Pierce of Georgia. A majority of Congress wanted to send the Constitution to the states with a recommendation that it be ratified. The minority was willing to send it along, but only with a cautionary note that Congress had no power to create a new confederacy. A compromise was reached. The members unanimously agreed to send the document to the states without any recommendation or note, leaving it to the states to act.

The struggle over ratification took place in two forums, the first being the press. On September 19, only two days after adoption of the Constitution, the *Pennsylvania Packet*, in Philadelphia, printed the text. Other newspapers all over the thirteen states printed the Constitution, too, as soon as they received it. The press was thereafter filled with articles by writers who adopted names like "Caesar" or "Constant Reader"—as was the custom of the day—to sign their contributions arguing for or against the Constitution.

One ancient name stood out from the rest—"Publius," whose articles appeared in New York newspapers between October 1787 and May 1788. In all, eighty-five articles signed by "Publius" were published, and these became known as *The Federalist Papers*. They were written by Hamilton, Madison, and John Jay, a leading political figure in New York. Hamilton wrote fifty-one, Madison twenty-six, and Jay five, and Hamilton and Madison jointly three. Today, *The Federalist* is considered a masterly explanation of the Constitution and a basic source of constitutional data. In their own day, however, the papers, although widely reprinted, did not cause much stir because they were too learned for the average reader.

But the contests to ratify the Constitution in the state conventions were spirited and hotly fought. The first came up in Pennsylvania, in the same chamber where the Constitution had been written. Thomas Mifflin, one of the delegates, read it aloud to members of the state legislature on September 18, the day after its adoption. Ten days later when George Clymer, who also had been a delegate, rose to propose a state convention for ratification, Anti-Federalists objected. Why not wait for the new legislature due to be elected in November, they demanded.

The Federalists, though, were for immediate action. To thwart them, Anti-Federalists stayed away the day a vote was scheduled, forcing its postponement for lack of a quorum. The next day, the sergeant at arms was sent to find the absentee members. Aided by a mob, he seized two assemblymen and carried them, fighting, to the State House. There, they were forcibly put into their seats. With a quorum achieved in that violent manner, the question of calling a convention to approve the Constitution was voted, forty-five to two.

Despite the speed with which Pennsylvania acted, it turned out not to be the first state to ratify the Constitution. That honor fell to Delaware. Once the citizens of that small state felt assured of having an equal vote in the new Senate, opposition to the Constitution had melted away. On December 7, meeting in Dover, delegates to Delaware's convention ratified the Constitution by a unanimous vote.

In the continuing debate in Pennsylvania, the major argument of the opposition to the Constitution—one that was to be repeated throughout the other states—revolved around the omission of a Bill of Rights. Wilson, the only delegate to the Pennsylvania convention who had also been at the Constitutional Convention, defended the document as it stood. "The preamble to the proposed Constitution, 'We the people of the United States . . .' contains the essence of all the bills of rights that have been or could be devised," he insisted.

That did not satisfy John Smilie. "It is not enough to reserve to the people a right to alter and establish a government," he said, "but some criterion should be established by which it can easily and constitutionally ascertain how far the government may proceed and when it transgresses its jurisdiction."

After five weeks of debate, on December 12, the Pennsylvania convention voted, forty-six to forty, to ratify the Constitution. That close vote was a sign of what was to come. For the nation turned out to be split almost evenly between those who favored the Constitution and those who opposed it, as reflected in the sentiments of the delegates elected to the various state conventions. And their feelings were strong.

In Pennsylvania, a lot of anger was stirred by the speed with which its state convention had acted. At an outdoor rally where ratification was to be celebrated with a bonfire and speeches, a mob of Anti-Federalists rushed toward the fire, and a battle of stones, fists, and clubs followed. The rioters put a torch to a copy of the Constitution, then burned a rag figure labeled "Wilson."

Meanwhile, New Jersey—also reassured as Delaware had been by gaining an equal voice in the Senate—had ratified the Constitution unanimously. Then on January 2, 1788, Georgia, too, ratified it unanimously. George Washington was not surprised by the action. "If a weak state with Indians on its back and Spaniards on its flank does not see the necessity of a general government there must I think be wickedness or insanity in the way," he wrote to a friend.

But Georgia's was the last unanimous vote for the Constitution. The next state to consider it, Connecticut, met in January in Hartford. With no serious opposition, the new charter was ratified by a vote of 128 to 40. In the state conventions that followed, though, the division was deep, the feelings bitter, and in some states the vote was extremely close.

Soon it was the turn of Massachusetts, a state regarded as strongly Anti-Federalist, where only two years earlier Shays's Rebellion had shaken the foundation of government. Citizens of Massachusetts were used to government by town meetings at which any man could have his say. They distrusted all delegated authority, all legislatures. As befitting a state with a strong democratic tradition, it elected a large number of delegates to its ratification convention—350.

John Hancock, the governor of the state and the man whose strong signature led all the rest on the Declaration of Independence, was elected chairman. Despite that honor, Hancock, who had a great sense of his own importance, was not sure of his position regarding the Constitution. He stayed away from the opening days of the convention, giving gout as his excuse, until he could find out the prevailing feeling among the delegates.

These included judges, clergymen, and members of the state legislature, most of whom favored the Constitution. Also present were farmers and rural residents, most of whom opposed it. Twenty-nine of the delegates had been among those who fought for or supported Captain Shays in the recent rebellion. They were still suspicious of state officials. Among the strong supporters of the Constitution were Nathaniel Gorham, Rufus King, and Caleb Strong, all of whom had been delegates to the Constitutional Convention.

Day after day, the men of Massachusetts debated the Constitution, clause by clause. The state had instructed its delegates to Philadelphia to insist on the annual election of members of the national legislature. Why, then, were they to be chosen every two years? The question came from Samuel Adams, who had been a firebrand during the Revolutionary War. Strong explained that it had been a necessary compromise. "I am satisfied," said Adams.

But the most dramatic exchange at the convention came between two farmers. Amos Singletary from Worcester County started it:

"Those lawyers, and men of learning, and money men who talk so finely and gloss over matters so smoothly, to make us poor illiterate people swallow down the pill, expect to get into Congress themselves," he said. "They expect to be the managers of this Constitution, and get all the power and all the money into their own hands. And then they will swallow up all us little fellows, like the great Leviathan, Mr. President. Yes, just as the whale swallowed up Jonah."

The reply came from Jonathan Smith from Lanesboro in western Massachusetts, who had witnessed at first hand the turmoil of Shays's Rebellion. He used a homey example to illustrate his support of the new Constitution:

"Brother farmers, let us suppose a case now. Suppose you had a farm of fifty acres and your title was disputed, and there was a farm of five thousand acres joined to you that belonged to a man of learning, and his title was involved in the same difficulty. Would you not be glad to have him for your friend, rather than stand alone in the dispute? Well, the case is the same. These lawyers, these moneyed men, these men of learning, are all embarked in the same cause with us, and we must all swim or sink together. And shall we throw the Constitution overboard because it does not please us alike?

"Some gentlemen say, don't be in a hurry. Take time to consider, and don't take a leap into the dark. I say take things in time, gather fruit when it is ripe. There is a time to sow and a time to reap. We sowed our seed when we sent men to the Federal Convention. Now is the harvest. Now is the time to reap the fruit of our labor. And if we don't do it now, I am afraid, we shall never have another opportunity."

Still, the outcome was in doubt. The Federalist strategists came up with a plan that they thought would win over some of the dissidents. They prepared a series of nine amendments—similar to the eventual Bill of Rights—limiting the power of the national government. And they thought that the undecided Hancock was just the man to introduce these proposed amendments as a compelling new reason for supporting the Constitution.

A political deal was made. Hancock agreed to present the amendments and support ratification. In return, the Federalists promised that "if Virginia does not unite, which is problematical, he [Hancock] is considered the only fair candidate for President." In short, if Washington was not going to be the first President, they would support Hancock.

And so on January 20 Hancock, his gout-swollen feet wrapped in bandages, was carried up the aisle to the chair of the presiding officer. He proposed adoption of the nine amendments. For days, the new clauses were debated. Finally, they were adopted and the Constitution ratified on February 6 by a vote of 187 for, 168 against, a margin of only nineteen votes.

The delegates paraded from the meeting house to Faneuil Hall where, one newspaper of the day said, "the toasts given were truly conciliatory . . . all appeared willing to bury the hatchet of animosity." To prove that good fellowship prevailed, some Boston citizens composed new words they sang to the tune of "Yankee Doodle." Their song had thirteen verses, starting:

> Now politicians of all kinds
> Who are not yet decided
> May see how Yankees speak their minds
> And yet are not divided. . . .

Two more states quickly ratified the Constitution. In Annapolis, the Maryland convention voted for it on April 28, sixty-three to eleven. And in Charleston on May 23, South Carolina ratified it, 149 to 73. That made eight ratifying states, one short of the nine needed to put the Constitution into effect. New Hampshire delayed, while Virginia opened her ratification convention, with New York scheduled to start shortly after.

On June 21, New Hampshire finally voted, fifty-seven to forty-six, to ratify. That made the necessary nine states—and the new Constitution formally stood adopted. But everybody knew the United States could not exist without Virginia and New York. Besides being two of the largest states, their geographical position made their ratification essential if there were to be any real union.

Richard Henry Lee openly made this point at the Virginia convention. "The other states cannot do without Virginia," he said, "and we can dictate to them what terms we please." But Patrick Henry was the major leader of the anti-Constitution forces there. Known everywhere for his oratory, he had electrified the thirteen colonies just before the American Revolution with his words, "If this be treason, make the most of it," and "Give me liberty or give me death." A former governor of Virginia, he opposed the Constitution because he thought it would limit the powers of his state, and he felt deeply that his first loyalty was to Virginia.

"The Constitution is the severance of the confederacy," Henry said. "Its language, 'we the people' is the institution of one great consolidated national government of the people of all the states, instead of a government by compact with the states for its agents. The people gave the convention no power to use the name."

He was answered by Randolph, who had flip-flopped once more, angering the Anti-Federalists counting on his support. The man who had introduced the Virginia plan into the Constitutional Convention now admitted his error in not signing the Constitution. "The question is now between union and no union," he said, "and I would sooner lop off my right arm than consent to the dissolution of the union."

Mason, who had also declined to sign the Constitution in Philadelphia, stood firm, though. "It is a national government," he said. "It is ascertained by history that there never was one government over a very extensive country without destroying the liberties of the people."

Still, the pro-Constitution forces were growing strong and their opponents weak because they had no positive plan to offer in its place. Washington, although he did not attend the Virginia convention, openly favored ratifying, and his example was enough for some. Madison defended the Constitution against all attacks, patiently answering criticisms. He was joined in arguments for the Constitution by George Wythe, one of the most respected lawyers in Virginia.

Here—as in Massachusetts—the pro-Constitution strategists, led by Madison, took some of the arguments away from their opponents by including a provision calling for a Bill of Rights along with their motion to ratify the Constitution. On June 25, before the delegates knew that New Hampshire had become the ninth state to ratify, they voted. Despite Madison's concessions it was close, with eighty-nine for and seventy-nine against.

That night angry Anti-Federalists held a mass meeting, with Henry presiding. He had done his best against the Constitution in the proper forum, the convention, he told the crowd. But now the question was settled. "As true and faithful republicans, you had all better go home now," he advised them, and they did.

News of Virginia's ratification reached New York on July 2. The New York delegates had been holding their ratification convention in Poughkeepsie for the past two weeks. The opposition in the state, led by Governor Clinton, was stronger than in any state that had so far met and seemed assured of a majority. Clinton was chairman of the convention, but he himself did not speak very often. His forces were led by a self-taught merchant with the odd name of Melancton Smith.

Hamilton led the advocates for the Constitution, assisted by Robert R. Livingston, the chancellor of the State Supreme Court, and John Jay. If New York did not join the Union, Livingston said, how could it possibly defend itself against the British to the north, in Canada, and the other states to the east and south? Yet it was Hamilton, with his experience at the Constitutional Convention and in the writing of *The Federalist*, who turned the tide in Poughkeepsie.

To the persistent calls by the Anti-Federalists for a second convention, which was their method of defeating the Constitution, Hamilton replied: "Let a convention be called tomorrow. Let them meet twenty times, nay twenty thousand times, they will still have the same difficulties to encounter, the same clashing interests to reconcile." The whole point of the Constitution, he said, was to preserve the rights of the states and still answer the purposes of the Union.

Hamilton's arguments were so persuasive that he was even able to convince Melancton Smith to vote for the Constitution—after the news from Virginia arrived. So the New York convention turned out to be a triumph for Hamilton personally, providing the solid basis for his lasting fame as a founding father.

Three days before the ratification vote, when the Anti-Federalist forces seemed to sense defeat, a parade in New York City was led by a float in the shape of a ship called the *Hamilton*. Twenty-seven feet long and ten feet wide, it was manned by thirty uniformed sailors and drawn by ten horses. After firing thirteen guns, one for each state, as a signal for beginning the march, the horse-drawn ship proceeded up Broadway. It stopped near Beaver Street, signaling for a pilot.

From the pilot boat came a voice: "Where bound?"

"To the new Constitution."

Still, the vote on July 26 in Poughkeepsie was extremely close, thirty in favor and twenty-seven against. The Anti-Federalists, who had started with a majority of the delegates, had been split wide open by Virginia's example and by Clinton's failure to lead them effectively. Some of the Anti-Federalists came around because they feared a possible secession from the state by the southern counties, which favored the new Constitution. Some worried about their own political futures. And some were won over to the federal cause by acceptance of a proposal expressing "full confidence" that amendments to the Constitution would be made to protect the rights of the states and their citizens.

With New York's ratification, the successful beginning of the new nation was now assured, although two of the original thirteen states, North Carolina and Rhode Island, held out. Both states had printed large amounts of paper money and were worried about what would happen to it under a national government.

In its first vote, North Carolina became the first state to reject the Constitution. On August 2, 1788, it voted 183 to 84 to defer action until a second convention considered a Bill of Rights. However, influenced by steps in the new Congress toward this goal, it voted again on November 21, 1789, and ratified the Constitution, 194 to 77.

Rhode Island, the only state that had refused to send any representatives to the Constitutional Convention, remained out of the Union until 1790. Seven times its legislature rejected motions to hold a convention to ratify the Constitution. Under threats of secession by Providence, its largest

city, and other towns, the legislature finally did call a convention. It ratified the Constitution on May 29, 1790, more
than a year after Washington took office as the first President, by the narrow vote of thirty-four to thirty-two. It thus
became the last of the original thirteen states to ratify the
Constitution.

5

The Bill of Rights

THE TRANSITION BETWEEN THE OLD "UNITED STATES in Congress Assembled" and the new United States under its newly-adopted Constitution was remarkably smooth. The last Continental Congress approved the election of the new members of the House of Representatives and the Senate. It also provided for the election of the first President of the United States in this way:

> Resolved that the first Wednesday of January next, be the day for appointing electors in the several states, which before said day shall have ratified the Constitution; that the first Wednesday in February next be the day for the electors to assemble in their respective states, and vote for a President; and that the first Wednesday in March next, be the time, and the present seat of Congress the place, for commencing proceedings under the said Constitution.

And so it went. The electors duly met in the states and voted for George Washington as the first President, which had been expected by everybody. But bad roads and bad weather kept Congress from meeting on March 4, 1789, in New York City as scheduled. It was not until April 6 that the two houses assembled to count the electoral votes.

Each of the sixty-nine electors had two votes. As expected, each of them had voted for Washington for President, and he was elected unanimously. John Adams of Massachusetts received the next highest number of votes, thirty-four, and was elected Vice President.

Immediately, John Langdon of New Hampshire, who had been chosen temporary president of the Senate, wrote a letter to Washington. Charles Thomson, the secretary of Congress, set out to deliver this message, which said:

> I have the honor to transmit to your excellency, the information of your unanimous election to the office of President of the United States. Suffer me, Sir, to indulge the hope that so auspicious a mark of public confidence will meet your approbation, and be considered a sure pledge of the affection and support you are to expect from a free and enlightened people.

On his arrival in Mount Vernon on April 14, Thomson found Washington at work as usual on his farm there. Washington was not surprised by this new summons. After reading the letter informing him of his election, he replied in his usual dignified way:

> Sir, I have long been accustomed to entertaining so great a respect for the opinion of my fellow citizens, that the knowledge of the unanimous suffrages having been given to my favor scarcely leaves me the alternative for an option. Whatever may have been my private feelings and sentiments, I believe I cannot give a greater evidence of my sensibility for the honor they have done than by accepting the appointment.

Two days later, Washington left Mount Vernon for New York. His journey was a triumphal procession, as the American people everywhere on his route greeted him with flags, parades, speeches, pealing bells, and gun salutes.

In Baltimore, Washington said he hoped to secure the liberties and promote the happiness of his fellow citizens. In Delaware, he promised to give preference to the produce and fabrics of America. In Philadelphia, he invoked God's help to prevent the nation from becoming "prey to anarchy or despotism." In Trenton, he was met by a party of women dressed in white, who sang an ode to "the mighty chief" who had rescued them from their foe.

But all those welcomes were overshadowed when Washington arrived at Elizabeth Town, New Jersey, just across the Hudson River from the city of New York. A barge fit for a king had been outfitted there, its awning adorned with crimson curtains. Thirteen experienced harbor pilots in handsome new white uniforms—each representing a state of the Union—rowed the barge across the river, escorted by festively decorated boats of every description. Aboard the barge was a female chorus singing:

> Hail thou auspicious day!
> Far let America
> Thy praise resound:
> Joy to our native land,
> Let every heart expand,
> For Washington's at hand,
> With glory crowned!

Ships, docks, and house roofs were crowded with people as the procession of barges and boats passed the Battery at the tip of Manhattan Island. Washington landed at the foot of Wall Street, where a parade had been formed to escort him to his temporary home. One witness reported that "the streets were so crowded that you might have walked upon the peoples' heads for a great distance."

A week later, at noon on April 30, 1789, came the moment of the inauguration of the nation's first President. Washington, keeping his promise to support domestic manufactures, wore a plain brown homespun coat and knee breeches, white stockings, and black shoes with silver buckles. By his side, a steel-hilted sword gave even this simple costume a ceremonial distinction. His face bore its usual expression of calm dignity, and his hair had been powdered as was the custom among gentlemen of the era, then tied back in a queue.

Washington stepped forward on the balcony of the Federal Hall, overlooking Wall Street. He rested his hand on a Bible, and repeated the oath of office read to him by Chancellor Robert R. Livingston of New York: "I do solemnly swear that I will to the best of my ability preserve, protect, and defend the Constitution of the United States."

Then Livingston cried out, "Long live George Washington, President of the United States!" And a great cheer arose from the crowd in the street below.

In his inauguration address, Washington urged Congress to move swiftly to propose constitutional amendments showing "a reverence for the characteristic rights of freemen and a regard for public harmony." It was a reminder that scarcely was needed. For every member of Congress knew very well that the Constitution had been ratified only because of promises that a Bill of Rights would be added to it.

Accordingly, on June 8, 1789, James Madison, now a Representative in the first Congress under the Constitution, arose on the floor of the House of Representatives and moved that it take up the matter of constitutional amendments. As he considered himself bound in honor and in duty, he said, "I shall proceed to bring the amendments before you as soon as possible. . . ."

In making this promise, Madison was acting for himself and other Federalists who had initially opposed a Bill of Rights at the Constitutional Convention but later changed their policy. During the ratification fights in several states, the Federalists had committed themselves to add guarantees of the rights of individuals to the Constitution and to confirm the states in the powers that were not delegated to the new national government.

The Bill of Rights that Madison subsequently proposed contained nine amendments changing words already in the Constitution, besides adding a new preamble that could have been taken directly from the Declaration of Independence. He moved:

> That there should be prefixed to the Constitution a declaration—that all power is originally vested in, and consequently derived from the people.
>
> That government is instituted, and ought to be exercised for the benefit of the people. . . .
>
> That the people have an indubitable, unalienable and indefeasible right to reform or change their government, wherever it be found adverse or inadequate to the purposes of its institution.

His proposals, along with amendments suggested by some of the states, were referred to a committee of the House composed of one member from each of the eleven states that then comprised the Union. Making a few alterations in the text of Madison's amendments, the House committee also did one thing that was to make them into a true Bill of Rights. Instead of changing the text of the Constitution as

Madison had suggested, it voted to add the amendments as new and separate articles.

When the committee's report came before the full House, the debate there was almost the same as it had been in the Constitutional Convention. Nobody was really against the idea of protecting the rights of the people and of the states against intrusion by the central government. But opponents felt that specified guarantees were unnecessary, that the entire Constitution was a guarantee of the rights of the people.

Following the debate, the House voted on August 24 to approve the amendments in the form of seventeen separate articles to be added to the Constitution. When the House proposals came before the Senate, it reduced the number to twelve by combining some of them. A conference committee of both chambers met to resolve the minor differences. Two men who had been intimately involved in writing the Constitution drafted the final version of the Bill of Rights— Madison, acting for the House, and Oliver Ellsworth of Connecticut for the Senate.

The rewritten Bill of Rights, consisting of the twelve amendments, was accepted by both the House of Representatives and the Senate. Shortly afterward, President Washington sent copies of the amendments to the states for ratification.

Under Article V of the Constitution, three-quarters of the states must ratify amendments before they take effect, either by the vote of the state legislatures or by state conventions called for the purpose. When the first amendments were proposed, the Union was made up of eleven states. With the admission of North Carolina, Rhode Island, and Vermont during the ratification period, the Union grew to fourteen states, thus requiring the vote of eleven states to make up the three-fourths majority required for ratification.

In the following three years, the state legislatures voted on the proposed amendments. But many of them rejected the first two proposed by Congress. One would have regulated the number of Representatives in Congress and the other would have barred any pay raises for Congressmen during their terms of office. Both were considered unnecessary.

But the states accepted the other ten as follows:

New Jersey	November 20, 1789
Maryland	December 19, 1789
North Carolina	December 22, 1789
South Carolina	January 19, 1790
New Hampshire	January 25, 1790
Delaware	January 28, 1790
New York	February 27, 1790
Pennsylvania	March 10, 1790
Rhode Island	June 7, 1790
Vermont	November 3, 1791
Virginia	December 15, 1791

With the vote of Virginia, the necessary three-fourths of the states had ratified the Bill of Rights.

And so the amendments originally proposed as Articles Three to Twelve became the first ten amendments to the Constitution—the Bill of Rights, as we know it today. To most Americans, its familiar words are the heart of the Constitution, guaranteeing freedom of speech, freedom of the press, freedom of religion, protection against unreasonable search and seizure, the right to a trial by jury, and the right to due process of law. The full text of these famous clauses will be found, following the Constitution itself, on page 227.

It should be noted that everybody at the time understood

that the Bill of Rights protected citizens from infringements by the federal government, not by the states. Several decades after the Bill of Rights took effect, in 1833 a citizen claimed for the first time that one of its clauses provided protection for him from a state action. His claim produced a notable decision by the Supreme Court.

The issue arose in Baltimore when John Barron and his associates sued the city because it had diverted the flow of a stream in the course of street construction work, causing deposits of sand near their docks that made them unusable. To Barron, this was a violation of the Fifth Amendment, guaranteeing against the taking of private property for public use without due compensation.

When the case reached the Supreme Court, Chief Justice John Marshall ruled that the Bill of Rights, including the Fifth Amendment, had been intended "solely" as a limitation on the exercise of power by the national government and did not apply to the states. "If the framers of these amendments intended them to be limitation on the powers of the state governments, they would have . . . expressed that intention," he said. Since they had not, he ruled that the Supreme Court had no jurisdiction over the case, and it was dismissed.

It would take a Civil War, several more constitutional amendments, and a change in judicial thinking before that decision was reversed and the Bill of Rights was deemed applicable to actions by state governments.

As a footnote, it should be added that three of the original thirteen states—Massachusetts, Connecticut, and Georgia—did not ratify the Bill of Rights until the celebration of the one hundred and fiftieth anniversary of Washington's inauguration in 1939.

6

A Tie Vote

THE AMBITIONS OF FOUR PROMINENT MEN—John Adams, Thomas Jefferson, Alexander Hamilton, and Aaron Burr— clashed during the presidential election of 1800, one of the most complicated ever held throughout American history. While three were candidates—Adams, Jefferson, and Burr—Hamilton was not. Behind the scenes, though, Hamilton exercised the wiles of an astute politician, attempting to maintain his own power as a President-maker.

It was a most unusual election year. For the first and only time in American history, an incumbent President— Adams—was running against an incumbent Vice President—Jefferson. It was also the first election in which clearly recognized political parties competed. The Federalists, with Adams as their standard-bearer, opposed the Democratic-Republicans led by Jefferson.

The result was a stunning surprise that would bring about the adoption of a new amendment to the Constitution. The tally of ballots cast by the official presidential electors produced a tie vote—not between Adams and Jefferson, the opposing candidates seeking the nation's top office, but between Jefferson and Burr, who were running on the same ticket. Even Burr himself had expected to be considered only as Jefferson's Vice President.

Nevertheless, in those simpler days when the population of the United States barely exceeded four million people, politics had already become very complex. There were differences of political philosophy, of course. The conservative Federalists generally supported a strong and expanding national government, while the more liberal Democratic-Republicans attacked federal encroachments on the powers of the states. Overriding such issues, however, were clashes of personalities.

By 1800, political feuds were giving American politics a high charge of emotion. Adams and Jefferson, who once had been friends, were scarcely on speaking terms. Hamilton and Jefferson had regarded each other with deep suspicion ever since serving together in President Washington's cabinet, where they had defended opposing points of view tirelessly. And even if Hamilton and Adams were both leaders of the Federalist party, they disliked each other personally, besides differing politically.

But the bitterest feud of all was the one between Hamilton and Burr, although they seemed alike in many ways. Both had risen to the rank of lieutenant colonel during the Revolution while they were only in their early twenties, and since then both had become prosperous lawyers, with a great interest in politics.

Thus far, Hamilton's career had earned him much more renown. Beyond playing a major role at the Constitutional Convention of 1787 and writing most of *The Federalist Pa-*

pers, he had displayed a brilliant grasp of finance when President Washington appointed him Secretary of the Treasury. Even his political enemies conceded that his money policies had put the country on a sound economic basis.

Above all, though, Hamilton had served as the chief advisor to the nation's first President, convincing Washington to interpret the Constitution broadly and use the "implied" powers of the office. From this experience of behind-the-scenes influence, Hamilton had come to relish exerting control indirectly. Moreover, he was sufficiently a realist to perceive that he stood little chance of winning any important election himself.

To most people of his day, Hamilton's undoubted gifts as a statesman were shadowed by a cloud because his parents had not been married. His father was a Scottish merchant who fell in love with an Englishwoman living on the West Indian island of Nevis and then abandoned her and her son. Perhaps it was owing partly to this unhappy start in life that the young Hamilton had showed such a driving ambition to better himself after he landed in New York to study at King's College.

While serving on Washington's staff during the Revolution, Hamilton had met the daughter of the wealthy General Philip Schuyler, and she became his wife in 1780. If this was a marriage founded on warm affection, which surely appeared to be the case, it also made Hamilton a member of one of New York's most influential families. He enjoyed his new status, and no doubt it affected his political philosophy.

At the Constitutional Convention, he himself had summed this up frankly. "All communities divide themselves into the few and the many," he said. "The first are the rich and well-born; the other the mass of the people . . . turbulent and changing, they seldom judge or determine right. Give therefore to the first class a distinct, permanent share in the Government."

Now, at the age of forty-five, Hamilton had resumed his law practice in New York City—and he was also attempting to gain the undisputed leadership of the Federalist party. In this endeavor, he found his particular hindrance to be another born leader who both personally and politically repelled him.

Nearly 200 years later, Aaron Burr remains a fascinating puzzle. This man who almost became President of the United States had many of the attributes contributing to political success, among them a notably keen mind and the ability to speak convincingly. Moreover, he possessed an abundance of the mysterious quality by which a public figure attracts a loyal following. Charisma, future generations of Americans would call the kind of charm he exerted.

Yet coupled with so much positive talent was a reckless streak that caused Burr to act as if he were above the rules binding ordinary mortals. Despite his outstanding family— his father had been the second president of the College of New Jersey—the young Burr was known for "dissipating" while he was a student there. Still, he graduated at sixteen with high honors.

Merely winning eminence as a lawyer in New York City did not satisfy him. Since Hamilton firmly ruled the state's Federalists, Burr's push to reach the top command of the Democratic-Republicans automatically made them political foes. But a personal antagonism also began to fester after Burr prevented Hamilton's father-in-law from achieving a post he desired. On the surface, they managed to behave politely to each other. As early as 1785, though, private letters Hamilton wrote to his friends contained remarks about Burr so hostile that hatred is not too strong a word to use concerning them.

In 1791, Burr was named a United States Senator from New York. While holding this office, he attracted so much favorable attention that he received thirty electoral votes for President in the national election five years later. Even so, amid the intricate political maneuvering in his own state, he lost his bid for a second term in the Senate. Soon, however, he won a lesser post as a member of the state assembly.

With his compelling ambition, Burr started working to build his own political machine. Cannily, he secured the support of Tammany Hall, an association of mechanics and other tradesmen in New York City. Carefully organizing early in 1800, he was able to obtain a majority for his party in the state legislature that year, defeating Hamilton's forces. That assured the Democratic-Republicans of the state's electoral vote in the 1800 presidential election and made Burr himself a crucial figure.

In those days before presidential primaries or nominating conventions, candidates were chosen at meetings of members of Congress belonging to each of the parties. Among the Democratic-Republicans, there was no question about who should head their ticket—the current Vice President, Thomas Jefferson. Burr, with the important New York vote under his control, convinced his party's caucus to name him as Jefferson's successor in the vice presidency.

But the Federalists, despite their hold on the White House, were split.

The incumbent President Adams, though a Federalist, had taken some independent positions that defied other leaders of his party—especially on the urgent issue of war or peace with France. Led by Hamilton, most of the Federalists were strongly on the side of the English and against the French in the continuing war between these two countries. They even wanted the United States to help the English defeat France. But Adams had sought to keep the nation out of the conflict by a series of negotiations, which infuriated the more aggressive members of his party.

And so, when the time came for the Federalists to select their candidate for President in 1800, there was bitter opposition to Adams. Still, he had enough supporters to win the nomination. Hamilton, though, could not accept this majority decision, and instead backed the Federalist vice presidential candidate, Charles Cotesworth Pinckney, of South Carolina. Hamilton hoped Pinckney would be able to win most of the electoral votes in the South and enough in the North to give him a chance of winning the presidency, rather than just the lesser post for which he had been named.

In effect, Hamilton was trapped by his antagonism toward both Jefferson and Adams. Hamilton realized that should Pinckney fail, as was most likely, his own refusal to support Adams would give Jefferson the victory. But Hamilton decided he would rather have even Jefferson than a second term for Adams. "If we must have an enemy at the head of the government," he said, "let it be one whom we can oppose, and for whom we are not responsible . . . who will not involve our party in the disgrace of his foolish and bad measures."

None of the candidates that year campaigned for office in the style we know today. As was the custom then, they stayed at home receiving visitors and writing letters. All the campaigning was done by their supporters, who held meetings and filled the newspapers with all sorts of angry attacks. It turned out to be one of the bitterest struggles in American political history.

The Federalists charged that Jefferson had cheated people to whom he owed money, obtained property by fraud, robbed a widow of her estate, and acted cowardly during the Revolutionary War when he was governor of Virginia. They also labeled him an atheist. The Democratic-Republican claims concerning Adams were equally absurd. They called him a hypocrite, a criminal, a tyrant—they even spread the story that he planned to have one of his sons marry one of King George III's daughters, thus starting an American monarchy.

There were, however, some serious issues as well. The Federalists warned that a Jefferson victory would wreck the economy and mean giving in to the French attacks on American commerce. The Democratic-Republicans denounced the Federalist "quasi-war" against the French and, more justifiably, the Federalist undermining of civil liberties by passage of the Alien and Sedition Acts.

All this was normal politics. The unusual aspect of the campaign came from the split in the Federalist party caused by Hamilton. Beyond his opposition to the Adams policy of negotiating with the French, Hamilton felt a personal resentment because Adams had refused to recognize him as the leader of the party. So he used some ill-considered words in a letter he sent to his supporters—urging them to vote for Pinckney as President, instead of Adams, on the grounds that Adams was "mean, petty, egotistic, erratic, and hot-tempered." Of course, the Democratic-Republicans promptly used this letter for their own purposes.

To the framers of the Constitution, a presidential election was a very important matter. They had erected a complex system whereby each state would select electors equal to the combined number of their Senators and Representatives in

Congress. In most states, the electors were chosen by the state legislatures, but in a few they were elected by the people. Each elector had two votes. When the electoral votes of all the states were counted, the person with the highest number of votes would become President and the one with the second highest Vice President.

That system had worked well in 1789 and 1792, when Washington had been elected unanimously, with Adams becoming Vice President. In 1796, the first contested presidential election, the results had been close but clear—Adams received seventy-one electoral votes, Jefferson sixty-eight, Thomas Pinckney of South Carolina fifty-nine, and Burr thirty. Adams became President and Jefferson Vice President, even though they represented opposing political parties.

By then, though, it was obvious that the framers of the Constitution had not foreseen the rise of political parties and had underestimated the intensity of partisan feelings. They had intended the electors to use their independent judgment in electing the President. But it was already apparent that electors considered themselves bound to vote for the candidate of the political party they represented.

In those days before voting machines and television reports made results almost immediate, the election returns became known only slowly. On November 27, Jefferson arrived back in Washington to take up his duties as Vice President without knowing whether he had been elected President or would soon retire to Monticello as a private citizen.

By mail and by courier on horseback, the election returns finally began to reach Washington in December. Toward the end of the month, an unofficial tally disclosed a most upsetting state of affairs: Jefferson had seventy-three electoral votes, Burr also had seventy-three, Adams sixty-five, Pinckney sixty-one, and John Jay one.

The men who wrote the Constitution had foreseen possible problems. They had provided that, if any candidate did not have a majority, it would be up to the House of Representatives to choose the winner. Behind the scenes, all sorts of maneuvering ensued.

On the Democratic-Republican side, Jefferson himself wrote to Burr and said he regretted not having arranged in advance for some of the electors to refrain from voting, which would have prevented the tie. Burr, in his reply, appeared to accept the secondary role: "My personal friends are perfectly informed of my wishes on the subject and can never think of diverting a single vote from you—on the contrary, they will be found among your most zealous adherents. I see no reason to doubt of your having at least nine states if the business should come before the House of Representatives."

For Hamilton, as leader of the Federalists, the prospect of having the House decide the issue created a serious dilemma. He opposed Jefferson because he disliked his political ideals. But by now he hated Burr passionately. So he sent letters to his colleagues denouncing Burr as a man "without probity" who "would not hesitate to sell his country for foreign gold." He tried to convince them that Jefferson was the lesser of two evils.

Even though Hamilton called Jefferson "a contemptible hypocrite," he wrote to Senator Gouverneur Morris: "I trust the Federalists will not finally be so mad as to vote for Burr. I speak with an intimate and accurate knowledge of his character. His elevation can only promote the purposes of the desecrate and profligate. If there is a man in the world I ought to hate, it is Jefferson. With Burr I have always been personally well. But the public good must be paramount to every private consideration."

Nevertheless, the Federalists in Congress decided to back Burr—even if he himself did not consent. To them, his position was the same as it had been in his letter to Jefferson and other associates when he had said he would not secretly connive to gain the presidency. Still, although Burr did not take any step to promote his own candidacy, neither did he do anything to encourage his supporters to vote instead for Jefferson.

On February 11, 1801, in an atmosphere of tension, while a snowstorm raged outside, a joint session of Congress met to count the electoral votes officially. As provided for in the Constitution, the Vice President—Jefferson—sat in the chair of the president of the Senate while the votes to decide his own future were counted. The outcome was precisely as expected: a tie vote, with seventy-three for both Jefferson and Burr.

As a result, the election was thrown into the House of Representatives where, under the rules set by the Constitution, a majority vote of nine of the sixteen states, with each state voting as a unit, was necessary to decide the winner. The first tally proved indecisive. Jefferson got eight states— New York, New Jersey, Pennsylvania, Virginia, North Carolina, Kentucky, Georgia, and Tennessee. Six states—New Hampshire, Massachusetts, Rhode Island, Connecticut, Delaware, and South Carolina—cast their ballots for Burr. Two states—Maryland and Vermont—were tied within their own delegations and so voted for neither candidate.

In the cold, unheated chamber of the House, its members continued to vote, time after time. From one o'clock in the afternoon, all through the night until eight o'clock the next morning, twenty-seven separate ballots were taken. All had the same results, eight states for Jefferson, six for Burr, two blank. Not one delegate or one state had changed. After the thirty-third ballot, the weary legislators decided to adjourn over the weekend.

That weekend, there were several private meetings. It was reported that some Federalists approached Burr and attempted to make a deal with him. But, as one wrote later, Burr rejected any deal and lost his chance to become President. Other Federalists sent an intermediary to meet with Jefferson and try to reach an understanding with him. Jefferson later denied that any bargain was made.

But when the House reconvened after the weekend, a few Federalist votes changed. In Maryland and Vermont, some congressmen who had voted for Burr now cast blank ballots, with the result that their states went for Jefferson. On the thirty-sixth ballot, Jefferson had ten states, one more than the nine required, and was declared the next President.

The transition of power from one political party to the other, the first such transfer in the United States, went peacefully but with extreme bitterness. The Federalists, who still controlled Congress, hastily passed two judiciary acts creating many new judges in the federal courts and justices of the peace in the District of Columbia. In his famous "midnight appointments," Adams filled the vacancies with faithful Federalists.

The bitterness was personal as well as political. Years earlier, Adams and Jefferson had worked together on the adoption of the Declaration of Independence. While abroad in London and Paris as ministers to England and France, they had corresponded warmly and helped each other. Abigail Adams, for example, had bought shirts for Jefferson in London, while he bought shoes for her in Paris. But in 1801

Adams was deeply hurt by his defeat. On the morning of the inauguration of his old friend, he left Washington without extending to him the bare courtesies of an outgoing President to his successor.

In that atmosphere of strain, Jefferson became the first President to take the oath of office in the new "federal city" of Washington. On the platform with him were Vice President Burr, who had just vied with him for the presidency, and the new Chief Justice, John Marshall, whom Adams had just appointed to be sure of having a sound Federalist heading the Supreme Court.

Jefferson tried in his inaugural address to smooth over the partisan bitterness. "We are all Republicans, we are all Federalists," he said, calling for unity in the years ahead.

At least on one matter, almost everyone agreed. It was that a constitutional change was needed to prevent a recurrence of the recent disputed election. Other pressing problems intervened, though, and not till 1803 did Congress propose the Twelfth Amendment.

This called for two separate elections by the electoral college, first choosing the President and then the Vice President. Since the necessity for such a change had been so clearly demonstrated, the ratification process went forward with little dissent. Curiously, however, both Delaware and Connecticut rejected the amendment because they feared it would diminish their power in electing a President. Yet by the middle of 1804, a sufficient number of states had ratified the Twelfth Amendment for it to become part of the Constitution in time for the presidential election later that year.

Jefferson ran again then, this time without Burr, and easily won a second term. Burr was nominated for governor of New York, but opposed by Hamilton as well as factions within his own party, he lost the contest.

Once again during this campaign, Hamilton was free in his criticism of Burr. Some letters were published in which Hamilton was quoted as having called Burr "a dangerous man who ought not be trusted with the reins of government."

Burr demanded that Hamilton retract his statements, putting Hamilton in a quandry. He either had to repudiate his words or face a duel, still the customary way gentlemen settled their differences. Reluctantly, Hamilton accepted the challenge to a duel despite his own deep disapproval of a practice that had already taken the life of his cherished eldest son.

At dawn on the morning of July 11, 1804, Aaron Burr and Alexander Hamilton faced each other, pistols in hand, on a field in Weehawken, New Jersey, just across the Hudson River from New York City. Each man fired a shot. Hamilton fell, mortally wounded.

Burr fled southward to escape prosecution for taking part in a duel, for this sort of violence was already illegal even if laws against it had not been taken too seriously. Ironically, it was the death of the esteemed Hamilton that shocked the nation into making sure dueling ceased.

Meanwhile, Burr returned to Washington to preside over the next session of the Senate in 1805. There his dignified conduct won praise even from some of his enemies, but soon it became obvious that his political career was finished. Then he embarked on one of the most bizarre adventures in the history of the American Southwest.

It was, apparently, an attempt to seize Mexico by force from Spain, which then owned it. Did he, or did he not, conspire to separate some of the western states from the Union as part of his scheme? There were people who thought so, and he was tried for treason. Although a jury acquitted him, Burr soon faded into obscurity.

The fourth player in the political melodrama that had led to the adoption of the Twelfth Amendment—grumpy John Adams—had returned to his home in Quincy, Massachusetts, in 1801. After Jefferson retired from the presidency, he and Adams mellowed sufficiently to renew their old friendship by exchanging letters for many years, although they never met again face to face. By a notable coincidence, they both died on the same date—July 4, 1826, the fiftieth anniversary of the Declaration of Independence, which they had both done so much to bring about.

7

John Marshall's Court

WILLIAM MARBURY, a clerk in the Navy Department back in 1801, is still remembered because of a job he failed to get. The outgoing President Adams, on his last night in the White House, had signed papers appointing Marbury and forty-one other loyal Federalists as justices of the peace for the city of Washington. But in all this haste to thwart the incoming President Jefferson, the document that would have made Marbury's job official was not delivered to him. As a result, he started a lawsuit that has kept at least his name from being forgotten.

For the suit turned out to be one of the landmark cases in United States constitutional history. It also marked the beginning of John Marshall's remarkable thirty-four-year career as the Chief Justice of the United States—a career that firmly established the Supreme Court as the nation's final interpreter of the Constitution.

Since Marshall's time, the Constitution has changed—

grown, as some put it—in two ways. One way has been through amendment, but in 200 years the Constitution has been amended only twenty-six times, with ten of those additions constituting the Bill of Rights. The second and more extensive way the Constitution has been changed has been by judicial interpretation.

Nowhere in the Constitution itself is the power to interpret the document explicitly given to the Supreme Court. Article III provides only that "The judicial Power of the United States, shall be vested in one supreme Court, and in such inferior Courts as the Congress may from time to time ordain and establish." It further specifies that the Supreme Court has original jurisdiction over all cases involving ambassadors and consuls of foreign countries, and those in which any state is a party, and that it can hear appeals in other cases.

Yet ever since John Marshall's day, the exercise of that judicial power has brought much controversy. The Supreme Court's increasing impact on the daily life of Americans, by its assumption of the right to declare laws constitutional or unconstitutional, has aroused strong political passions, both for and against the court. Presidents, members of Congress, and ordinary citizens have all felt intensely about various of the court's opinions.

Even the court itself has not been immune to outside political pressure—or the influence exerted by the political philosophies of its members. Over the years, there have been times when the court's conservative leanings have led to dissension, for instance during the administration of President Franklin D. Roosevelt, as Chapter Twelve will relate. There have also been times when its liberal decisions have brought a great outcry among the conservative-minded, as will be seen in Chapter Thirteen.

Chief Justice John Marshall in a painting by J.W. Jarvis. *Courtesy Carter, Ledyard & Milburn and the Frick Art Reference Library*

Still, the words of the Constitution itself have not changed, apart from the comparatively few amendments. But the court's interpretation of the document's meaning has certainly changed, usually in the direction of broadening it to encompass new times and new situations. As Chief Justice Charles Evans Hughes once said, "We live under a Constitution, but the Constitution is what the judges say it is."

Back in 1793, only four years after the United States came into being, the Supreme Court had found itself embroiled in passionate politics under its first Chief Justice, John Jay. That year, the court had ruled in the case of *Chisholm v. Georgia* that the state could be sued by a nonresident for the payment of debts, citing the provision of Article III in the Constitution giving the federal courts jurisdiction over controversies between a state and a citizen of another state or a foreign country.

But Georgia, furious at what it saw as an invasion of its sovereignty, passed a law providing that "any federal marshal, or any other person, seeking any state property under *Chisholm v. Georgia,* shall be guilty of felony and shall suffer death, without benefit of clergy, by being hanged." Georgia was not alone in its opposition to the Supreme Court decision. Other states, among them New York, Massachusetts, and Maryland, also were eager to end the danger of being compelled to pay their debts by a federal court.

Within a year, a constitutional amendment had been drawn up by Congress to reduce the power of the federal judiciary. The Eleventh Amendment, ratified by the states in 1794, held:

> The judicial power of the United States shall not be construed to extend to any suit in law or equity, commenced or prosecuted against one of the United States by citizens of another State, or by citizens or subjects of any foreign state.

That was a clear and explicit reversal of what the framers of the Constitution had written. The speed with which the Eleventh Amendment was passed indicated that when there was sufficient pressure in both Congress and the states to amend the Constitution, the elaborate procedures for doing so were no barrier. But the decision in the case of *Chisholm v. Georgia* had another meaning, too. It was a small step along the road that led to the broad assertions of the powers of the federal courts to interpret the Constitution, made a few years later by the Marshall Supreme Court.

At the Constitutional Convention and in the ratification fights, the evidence about what powers the framers meant to give the Supreme Court was contradictory. Professor Edwin S. Corwin, one of the leading authorities on constitutional law, has noted that people who say the framers intended the court to exercise judicial review—the power of ruling on the constitutionality of any law—"are talking nonsense." But, he quickly added, "and the people who say they did not intend it are talking nonsense."

Yet those who do believe that the Constitution provides for Supreme Court interpretation of the meaning of the document's words insist this power is clearly implied. They also find evidence in *The Federalist Papers*, in which Alexander Hamilton wrote that interpretation of the laws adopted under the Constitution was a proper function of the Supreme Court.

Although the court's role as the final arbiter of what the Constitution means has become generally accepted, the issue has been debated for 200 years and is still debated today. That argument started in 1801, when William Marbury's case came before the court. On the surface, it involved a simple question: Was Marbury entitled to his new job? But the case soon became the focus of a complicated political battle involving two Presidents and the Chief Justice.

Early in 1801, Adams was bitter about his defeat for a second term by his political enemy, Jefferson. When he heard that the office of Chief Justice was about to become vacant, Adams was determined that Jefferson would not make the new appointment. He called in his Secretary of State, John Marshall, and asked his advice. Marshall mentioned a name. No, said Adams. He looked at Marshall thoughtfully. "I believe I must nominate you," he said.

At that time, Marshall was a forty-six-year-old lawyer, a thin, tall man with clothes that never seemed to fit him. His face was plain, and he looked more like a country store-keeper than an important public figure. But despite his un-distinguished appearance, his ability to conceive of new legal principles when he was confronted with unprecedented kinds of cases would make even his political foes consider him a legal genius.

Born on the edge of the wilderness in Virginia, Marshall had never gone to school but learned to read and write from tutors and his father's library. For his family was not poor, and his father had been a childhood friend of George Washington. After fighting in the Revolutionary War, Marshall studied law at the College of William and Mary. When he became involved in politics, his intense belief in the importance of a strong national government made him a leading spokesman for the Federalist party in Virginia. That brought him into conflict with his distant cousin Thomas Jefferson, the head of the opposing Democratic-Republican party.

Indeed, Marshall had helped President Adams make all his "midnight appointments" of Federalists just before leaving office. Then, soon after Marshall moved to the Supreme Court, he turned out to be the man who decided to hear the case of *Marbury v. Madison*. In this suit, Marbury was seeking an order compelling the new Secretary of State, James Madison, to issue his commission as a justice of the peace.

Modern commentators say that Marshall, as an interested

party, should have excused himself from the case. But he did not do so because he was eager to demonstrate the power of the court over the executive branch of the government led by his political opponent, Jefferson. That attitude made Jefferson and his supporters even angrier. Already indignant over the last-minute appointments by Adams, now they felt that the court had no business interfering with the functions of the office of the President, which included making appointments.

A further complication was that the Marbury suit differed from the usual appeal to the Supreme Court from a lower court decision. It was brought directly to the highest court under a provision of the Judiciary Act of 1789, which had established the federal courts. One section of the law authorized the Supreme Court to issue writs to public officials, such as the one sought by Marbury. So, in 1803, the Supreme Court sat in an unusual session, hearing witnesses in the case of *Marbury v. Madison*.

After listening to the testimony, Marshall found himself in a dilemma. He knew that if he issued the writ ordering Madison to give Marbury the job, it probably would be ignored. That would make the court lose prestige and power. But his sense of justice combined with political partisanship had convinced him that Marbury was entitled to the job. Marshall found an inspired solution, which would strike future scholars as one of the cleverest of his career.

In his written opinion, Marshall solved his problem this way. He found that Marbury was entitled to his commission and sharply criticized the Jefferson administration for its unlawful failure to deliver it. But then he ruled that the Supreme Court did not have the power to compel Jefferson to issue the commission because of a technicality.

Marshall reasoned that, under the Constitution, the Supreme Court could issue such an order only in the case of an appeal from a lower court decision. He cited the constitutional provision that the Supreme Court had original jurisdiction only over cases involving ambassadors or those in which a state was a party. Since the Marbury case involved neither an ambassador nor a state, the section of the Judiciary Act that gave him the right to go directly to the Supreme Court violated the Constitution and was, therefore, invalid.

"One of the fundamental principles of our society," said Marshall, "is that the Constitution controls any legislative act repugnant to it." Since it was the duty of the judiciary to say what the law was, he continued, the Supreme Court had the duty of overturning any law it deemed unconstitutional. "A law repugnant to the Constitution is void," he said.

With that decision, the Supreme Court for the first time held that a law passed by Congress could be considered invalid. Before then there had been a widespread assumption that the constitutionality of federal legislation would be a judicial question, but it had not been spelled out until Marshall actually said so.

Despite its importance, the Marbury decision was received quietly. Jefferson was upset, not by the principle of holding a law unconstitutional but at Marshall's criticism of him. Marbury himself disappeared from the scene and later became the president of a bank in Georgetown. There was no uproar in Congress, perhaps because at the time it did not seem like a historic ruling. It took more than half a century before the Supreme Court declared another law passed by Congress unconstitutional.

Following the Marbury case, one of the major questions faced by the Marshall court was whether it could declare a state law unconstitutional. The divisive issue of states' rights versus national rights was as old as the United States itself.

At the Constitutional Convention, one great split among the delegates had been between those who favored a strong national government and those eager to protect the rights of individual states. When the Bill of Rights was adopted, a primary reason had been to curb the powers of the national government and to preserve the powers of the states.

The Supreme Court faced the issue of states' rights squarely in a case involving land fraud in Georgia. Back in 1795 the state's legislature, influenced in part by bribery, had granted millions of acres along the Yazoo River to land companies, which sold some of the plots to settlers. At the next session of the legislature, Georgia changed its mind and rescinded the grant. Some of the innocent settlers sued to retain their land in the case of *Fletcher v. Peck* in 1810.

Handing down a decision his colleagues on the bench unanimously supported, Marshall issued a precedent-making ruling. He held that the Georgia law rescinding the grant violated the constitutional provision prohibiting a state from passing any law impairing the obligations of contracts. It was the first time that a state law was declared to be unconstitutional because it conflicted with a clause in the Constitution.

But that was not the final answer to the troublesome question of states' rights, which remained a major point of argument until the Civil War. Even in modern times, the issue would once more surface during the school desegregation crisis of the 1950s and 1960s and, to a certain extent, it is still with us today.

Back in 1821, the states' rights issue came before the Supreme Court again in a case involving a bank. James McCulloch was the cashier of the Baltimore branch of the Bank of the United States. When an agent of Maryland called on him to request payment of a new tax that the state had imposed on the bank, McCulloch refused to pay. The state brought suit against the bank in the state courts and won, as expected. The bank appealed.

Few cases before the Supreme Court aroused such passion as the bank case. To farmers, the bank was a symbol of oppression because it controlled their money. Many state bankers were against the Bank of the United States because it presented too powerful a competition. And then there were those who opposed it on political grounds, saying a national bank was unconstitutional because the Constitution did not give Congress the express power to charter banks or corporations.

When the case was argued in the Supreme Court, the two sides agreed on the facts. That left two major questions before the court. Was the bank constitutional? And, if so, did Maryland have the power to tax it?

In many ways, the arguments were a repeat of the debate between Hamilton and Jefferson at the time the first Bank of the United States had been considered during Washington's administration. To Hamilton, the Constitution was a document to be interpreted broadly, not restricting the President or Congress to just the powers specifically enumerated. For Hamilton, it was clear that the implied powers of the Constitution gave Congress the authority to establish a bank. To Jefferson, taking a single step beyond the powers delegated to Congress by the Constitution was not warranted. In the words of the Tenth Amendment, all rights not listed were "reserved to the states or to the people."

Four days after the *McCulloch v. Maryland* arguments ended, Marshall was ready with the court's decision. He acknowledged that establishing a bank was not among the powers enumerated for Congress in the Constitution. But, he added, it had been obviously impossible for the framers of the Constitution to list all the possible powers of Congress. To have done so, he said, would have made it a legal code, not a Constitution.

"We must never forget that it is a constitution that we are expounding," he said in a sentence that has been quoted frequently. That Constitution, he went on, gave Congress the additional power to make "all laws necessary and proper to carry into execution the foregoing powers, and all other powers vested by this Constitution in the government of the United States, or in any department thereof."

Therefore, Marshall concluded, the bank was a proper means to a legitimate end as seen by Congress. He added:

> We think the sound construction of the Constitution must allow to the national legislature that discretion, with respect to the means by which the powers it confers are to be carried into execution, which will enable that body to perform the high duties assigned to it, in the manner most beneficial to the people. Let the end be legitimate, let it be within the scope of the Constitution, and all means which are appropriate, which are plainly adapted to that end, which are not prohibited, but consist with the letter and spirit of the Constitution, are constitutional.

That meant that the bank was constitutional. The question remained, though, that even if it was, could Maryland tax it?

No, said Marshall, the power to tax is the power to destroy. He went on: "The states have no power, by tax or otherwise, to retard, impede, burden or in any manner control the operations of constitutional laws enacted by Congress to carry into execution the power vested in the central government. This is, we think, the unavoidable consequence of that supremacy that the Constitution has declared."

As a result, the court decided, the Maryland law taxing the bank was "unconstitutional and void."

Unlike the decision in *Marbury v. Madison,* the bank decision produced a loud popular outcry against the court. Despite the ruling, Ohio voted to tax the bank within its borders, just as Maryland had. Other states denounced the court but stopped short of going against the decision. Although the Supreme Court decided against Ohio, too, the issue of states' rights did not die.

Another important issue on which the Marshall Court took action involved the authority of Congress over the economic development of the nation. Today, that regulatory power is accepted as a matter of course, but early in the 1800s the assertion that Congress could pass laws affecting interstate commerce seemed quite daring. The decision came in a case involving the newly-invented steamboat—and like the steamboat itself, the decision was a pioneer.

It all began with a meeting in Paris between two Americans. One was Robert Fulton, an artist and inventor. He dreamed of developing a vessel that could travel under water and actually constructed a submarine that could do so. He also worked on plans to use steam power to propel a ship on the surface of the water. Yet Fulton himself did not invent the steamboat, he merely experimented with models and engines until he arrived at a combination that seemed commercially feasible.

In Paris, Fulton found a financial backer in Robert R. Livingston, one of the noted Livingstons from Clermont on the Hudson River in Columbia County, New York. A rich and well-connected landowner, Livingston had been the judge who administered the oath of office to George Washington in New York in 1789. Over a decade later, he was serving as the United States minister to France and conducting negotiations that resulted in the Louisiana Purchase of 1803.

Both Livingston and Fulton saw immense profits ahead with a successful steamboat that could carry freight as well as passengers in a growing and thriving America, using great waterways like the Hudson, Ohio, and Mississippi Rivers. With his powerful connections, Livingston took the first steps to assure their fortunes. He arranged to secure a monopoly on steamboat transportation on the Hudson River. Meanwhile, Fulton ordered a new steam engine to be built for him in England and shipped to the United States. In 1807, his brand-new steamboat was ready for its trial run.

On August 17, 1807, the vessel called the *Clermont* made its maiden voyage up the Hudson from New York to Albany. It was a long, slim boat, 150 feet in length by 13 feet wide, with paddle wheels at the sides driven by a steam engine in the center. As it steamed up the river at night, one farmer was reported to have marveled that "the Devil was going up to Albany in a sawmill."

With that triumphant voyage, the age of the steamboat arrived in the United States—and the Fulton-Livingston team had a monopoly on steam traffic on the Hudson. But as steamboating prospered, other businessmen entered the field and challenged this monopoly. The owners of a rival vessel started a competitive service between New York and Albany but were forced to stop by a state court. It held that the state could regulate all commerce within its borders, and thus the grant of the monopoly to Livingston was valid.

In the next few years, though, the situation grew much more complicated. Following the death of Livingston, his heirs granted a license to Aaron Ogden, a former governor of New Jersey, to operate a steamboat across the Hudson River between New York and New Jersey. Then a former partner of Ogden's named Thomas Gibbons started operating another steamboat in the same waters, in apparent violation of

Ogden's license. When Ogden obtained a state court decision ordering Gibbons to cease operating, Gibbons appealed
to the Supreme Court.

He argued that his vessels were licensed to sail under a
federal law regulating ships in the coastal trade. Therefore,
he said, he had the right to sail between New York and New
Jersey, despite the monopoly granted by New York to
Livingston. The case, *Gibbons v. Ogden*, was argued before
the Supreme Court in 1824.

In his decision, Chief Justice Marshall for the first time
defined what "commerce" meant in the constitutional clause:
"Congress shall have the power to regulate commerce with
foreign nations, among the several states, and with the Indian tribes." He ruled that commerce was not restricted to
buying and selling, but also included navigation.

So, according to Marshall, the grant of the steamboat monopoly in New York came in conflict with the federal law
licensing those engaged in the coastal trade. Therefore, the
state law was unconstitutional and invalid. Gibbons had won
his case—the Livingston monopoly was broken.

There were two effects. The immediate one was the rapid
explosion of steamboat commerce, contributing importantly
to the growth of the United States in the mid-nineteenth
century. The second was to set a pattern for Supreme Court
decisions in the future, expanding "the commerce clause" of
the Constitution while at the same time preventing states
from taking steps inconsistent with national policy.

In his thirty-four years as Chief Justice, Marshall wrote
519 opinions, almost half the number delivered by the entire
court during that period. Included among them were rulings
in major cases that laid the foundations for acceptance of the
Supreme Court as the final authority on what the Constitution means. One of his procedural innovations, that of having

one justice deliver the opinion of "the court"—instead of the earlier practice of each justice delivering his own opinion— made the court an institution, rather than just a collection of judges. As a result, Marshall would be credited with giving the court a moral force as great as that of the President and Congress.

Still active even as his health finally began to fail, Marshall died in 1835 at the age of eighty. Today he is widely regarded as the greatest of all Supreme Court justices, the man who shaped the court into the powerful force that it remains 200 years after the nation's birth.

8

The War Amendments

THE MAN WHO SUCCEEDED MARSHALL as Chief Justice came from a wealthy Maryland family of tobacco growers. Roger B. Taney had freed his own slaves, but throughout his long career in politics and then on the Supreme Court he never lost his Southern loyalty. At the age of eighty, he issued a decision that made the Civil War almost inevitable.

It was his ruling in the intensely controversial Dred Scott case. Even some basic facts about this very complicated lawsuit have never been cleared up to the satisfaction of modern investigators. For instance, nobody knows how or why the suit actually started—and yet, the most important details can quickly be summarized.

Dred Scott was a slave owned by an Army medical officer named Emerson, who took him to a post out in Western territory that had not yet been organized into any state. By the terms of the famous Compromise of 1820, slavery was forbidden there.

103

Chief Justice Roger B. Taney, author of the Supreme Court's highly controversial D... d Scott decision, as seen by one of his contemporaries. *Courtesy New York Public Library Picture Collection*

Dr. Emerson was transferred a few years later to the slave state of Missouri, where Dred Scott soon emerged as the plaintiff in a series of legal actions aimed at securing his freedom. He claimed that his residence in a "free soil" area had permanently ended the bondage into which he had been born. At last, after more than ten years of involved maneuvering, the case reached the Supreme Court in 1857.

By then, it was no longer a question just of freeing one individual slave. According to some researchers, Dred Scott himself really had not had much to do with any of the proceedings, being an aging, good-natured man who never learned to read or write and died, practically unnoticed, about a year after the big furor raised in his name.

Apparently, a white anti-slavery advocate used him for the purpose of stirring public opinion—and the mounting dispute between the two sections of the country had reached such a pitch of emotion by 1857 that abolitionist forces rallied strongly behind his cause. Similarly, the South saw an opportunity for gaining a verdict that would stop any further Northern interference on a matter it believed the Constitution gave each state the right to deal with itself.

Considering the highly charged feelings swirling around the slavery issue, any decision on the Dred Scott case could hardly have avoided intensifying the North-South enmity. No doubt, the wisest policy would have been for the Supreme Court simply to refuse to hear it. And most experts say there were ample legal grounds to justify such a refusal.

Instead, though, Chief Justice Taney, in the quavering but convinced voice of an old Southern aristocrat, delivered an opinion that went far beyond any limited point of law he might have addressed—to infuriate even the least antagonistic Northerners.

Taney held, first of all, that Dred Scott should not have been allowed to institute any lawsuit because, as a Negro, he was not and could not under the Constitution be considered a citizen with the right to go into court, no matter what the circumstances.

Then Taney added a still more inflammatory pronouncement. He held that no claim could ever be made regarding emancipation as the result of residence in a free-soil area

An eighteenth-century artist's portrait of Dred Scott. *Courtesy New York Public Library Picture Collection*

established by the Compromise of 1820—because that law itself violated the Constitution. Specifically, the Chief Justice cited the following clause from the Fifth Amendment in the Bill of Rights:

No person . . . shall be deprived of life, liberty, or property, without due process of law. . . .

Amazing as it may seem, more than 100 years later, Chief Justice Taney saw no irony in using a clause forbidding the federal government to deprive any person of liberty as the basis for upholding slavery. In his eyes, the Constitution was a document applying only to white citizens, and the important word to him was "property." Since he thought of slaves as just another form of property, it struck him as sound reasoning that Congress lacked the power to deprive slaveowners of what belonged to them, merely because they chose to settle in an area under direct federal jurisdiction.

While the principle that the Supreme Court could declare any act of Congress unconstitutional had been accepted from the early days of Chief Justice Marshall's tenure, the court had never yet overturned any measure about which the nation felt strongly. So the Dred Scott decision brought a storm of protest from anti-slavery activists, and even from moderate-minded Northerners who felt that Chief Justice Taney had abused his high office by allowing his personal prejudices to influence his judgment. No matter that five other justices, four of them also Southerners, had concurred with their leader—and, at least temporarily, they would all be great heroes in the South—it was Taney's fate to bear the brunt of lasting disgrace.

In time to come, many authorities on the Constitution would agree that Taney deserved this censure. "A sorry episode in Supreme Court history," would be one of the milder verdicts about his conduct on the Dred Scott case. "The most disastrous opinion the Supreme Court has ever issued," a Harvard professor concluded a century afterward.

For the tempest created by the case did not subside. "If

the people obey this decision," one Northern newspaper asserted, "they disobey God." Such fury in the North only increased the Southern determination not to permit outside
"meddling" with its way of life—until, just four years later,
open warfare erupted between the two sections.

Following the Union victory in the Civil War, the Dred
Scott opinion continued to cause repercussions. It was one of
the prime factors contributing toward the passage of three
new constitutional amendments—the Thirteenth, Fourteenth, and Fifteenth. In the future, these would often be
referred to as "the war amendments."

Like the war itself, the constitutional changes associated
with it defy easy explanation because of the clouds of emotion obscuring facts and motives. Unquestionably, though,
the group in Congress known as the Radical Republicans was
responsible for pushing through this trio of amendments. So
it is helpful to know something about the personalities of its
two leaders, Senator Charles Sumner of Massachusetts and
Congressman Thaddeus Stevens of Pennsylvania.

Senator Sumner, standing six feet and four inches tall, had
a strong face and a voice of great power, which he had used
skillfully ever since his early years as a Boston lawyer. While
he could be charming to ladies he met at social events, his
political manner became extremely abrasive. Once, a colleague who had just listened to him deliver a blistering attack protested: "But you forget the other side." Sumner
crashed his fist on a table. "There *is* no other side!" he exclaimed.

Although Sumner's anti-slavery convictions won him
prominence as a spokesman for the abolitionists during the
1850s, his method of expressing them had led to one of the
least glorious moments in the annals of the United States
Senate. It was May of 1856 when he rose to speak in the

great debate over whether Kansas should be admitted to the Union as a slave or a free state. Hour after hour, he heaped insults on his political enemies, singling out Senator Andrew P. Butler of South Carolina as his special victim.

Butler, an elderly and courteous gentleman, was not on the floor then to make any reply. But two days later, a young cousin of his representing the same state in the lower house of Congress, strode up to Senator Sumner's desk, raised his cane, and beat him unconscious. More than three years would elapse following this assault by Congressman Preston Brooks before Senator Sumner felt well enough to resume the regular performance of his legislative duties. The terrible pain he suffered certainly did not soften his attitude toward the South.

Even if Thaddeus Stevens, Sumner's main ally, lacked any such personal grounds for bitter emnity, some people thought that his extreme harshness might be traced to a major property loss—the destruction of his ironworks during the Civil War fighting around Gettysburg. Others, though, who were more familiar with his whole career, believed the real explanation went much deeper.

Born in Vermont of a drunken father who had abandoned his family not long after his son's birth, Stevens was further handicapped by a misshapen foot that caused him to limp awkwardly. His mother did her best to protect him from the taunts of other children by encouraging him to read and study. Laboring as a nursemaid, she earned the money to send him to Dartmouth College.

There he did well in his classwork, but his prickly behavior brought him few friends. Of course, modern psychologists would point out that he must desperately have envied the good health and prosperous family connections of most of his classmates—for he set out as soon as he graduated to compel respect if not affection by becoming rich himself.

After moving to Pennsylvania, Stevens taught at country schools until he could afford to study law. Then, besides winning local renown for the burning intensity of his courtroom defense of poor clients, he accomplished his goal of making a lot of money by promoting railroads and manufacturing iron. His hatred for slavery finally landed him in politics, and he was soon elected to the House of Representatives.

Stevens was already sixty-seven in 1859 when he began attracting national attention. With the country on the brink of outright war, his fierce words about those who still wanted to seek some new compromise with the South fit the mood of many abolitionists. Said Stevens about one such speech: "As I heard it I could have cut his damned heart out."

During the actual fighting, "Old Thad" held the important post of chairman of the House Ways and Means Committee. But his own stern and positive views were constantly frustrated by President Lincoln's less aggressive policies. When Stevens received word about the assassination of Lincoln, one writer noted, "his sorrow was not keen."

Stevens and Sumner both felt then that Congress must assert itself decisively to set the terms on which the newly-defeated Southern states were readmitted to the Union. "With malice toward none" and "with charity toward all," Lincoln had pledged in his Second Inaugural Address "to bind up the nation's wounds." Unfortunately, hatred and vengeance would be substituted under the reconstruction policies pressed by the Radical Republicans.

Whether Lincoln himself could have prevented this if he had lived can never be answered. His weak yet well-meaning successor—Andrew Johnson, a backwoods Tennessee lawyer who had been a compromise candidate for Vice President—certainly proved unable to thwart those in Congress striving to punish the South by treating it like a conquered province. Because he did try, Johnson was subjected in 1868 to the humiliation of an impeachment and trial that very nearly succeeded, absolutely unjustifiably, in removing him from the White House.

While this whole sad chapter of American history can only be hinted at here, it does provide the background against which the war amendments must be considered. For these three additions to the Constitution were fundamental features of the Sumner-Stevens program—something like doses of medicine the South was forced to swallow before representatives from any formerly rebel states could be seated in Congress.

On the surface, all three appear to be entirely high-minded. Indeed, sooner or later some such guarantees of legal equality for blacks would surely have been necessary to protect them against unjust treatment. But even if the aim of the amendments may seem hardly disputable more than a century later, in the immediate aftermath of the Civil War—in the North as well as the South—racial prejudice was still so deeply ingrained that only dedicated reformers or calculating political cynics could expect mere words appended to the Constitution to accomplish much.

About the first of the new amendments, dissent had to be disguised. Many thousands of lives had been lost to end the evil of slavery, and the Thirteenth proclaimed:

> Neither slavery nor involuntary servitude, except as a punishment for crime whereof the party shall have been duly convicted, shall exist within the United States or any place subject to their jurisdiction.

This was proposed by Congress on January 31, 1865, a few months before the surrender of the Southern Confederacy when its defeat seemed imminent. But despite the overwhelming Northern revulsion against slavery, much of it religiously based, the adoption of even such an apparently uncomplicated addition to the Constitution was fraught with uncertainties.

Every previous amendment had, in one way or another, only altered governmental procedure or limited federal power. Now, however, an effort was being made to bring about a specific reform throughout the country. Was it, in fact, constitutional to use the amending process as a means to force any new restriction on all the states?

Much debate about this fine point occupied members of Congress. Because of the secession of the Southern states, many of the most vigorous defenders of the principle of states' rights before the war could no longer argue against federal interference. Still, even in a Senate and House composed solely of Northerners, fervent warnings concerning the proposal reverberated.

It was nothing short of revolutionary, some members cried. Allowing the national government to invade the area that the Constitution, as written, clearly reserved for the states would be altering the whole federal system, they insisted. At least in this respect, from the hindsight of history they were right—a new era of federal predominance did begin during these years.

Despite all such arguments, though, the required two-thirds of the membership of both houses found it possible to recommend this amendment abolishing slavery. They did so on the grounds that the Constitution itself set forth a procedure for amending any provision except the one regarding equal representation by all the states in the Senate. Thus, any amendment adopted by following the proper procedure would legitimately become as effective as the rest of the document.

That matter of "proper" procedure, nevertheless, created unprecedented problems. After the recommendation by Congress favoring the ban on slavery, affirmative votes by twenty-seven of the then thirty-six states were needed to complete the process of ratification. Yet in January 1865, with the Confederacy still unbeaten, there were only twenty-five states in the Union—including the border states of Kentucky and Delaware, where slavery continued to exist. Not surprisingly, these two rejected the proposed amendment.

Somehow, then, at least four of the eleven states that had seceded would have to vote in favor if the amendment were to be ratified. Amid all the confusion and upheaval accompanying the Southern surrender that April, the Congressional leaders promoting the constitutional change never ceased pressing ahead. Remarkably, they managed to secure approval from the legislatures of eight formerly rebel states by December 18, 1865, when the Thirteenth Amendment was formally proclaimed a part of the supreme law of the land.

But it was just one sign of the peculiar ethics prevailing then that the eight Southern ratifications came from the legislatures of new provisional governments, set up under a plan for healing the wounds of the war first proposed by President Lincoln. After Lincoln's tragic death, President Johnson attempted to carry out the same forgiving program in the face of furious opposition by Senator Sumner and Congressman Stevens.

And yet these same two men were the strongest sponsors of the Thirteenth Amendment. Still, if their conduct on this issue left them open to charges of hypocrisy, some much more lasting questions arose from the next constitutional addition they began pushing through the following year.

Again on the surface, the Fourteenth Amendment may

seem only a form of insurance to prevent any future Supreme Court verdict similar to the portion of the Dred Scott decision denying Negroes citizenship. For its first sentence declared:

> All persons born or naturalized in the United States, and subject to the jurisdiction thereof, are citizens of the United States and of the State wherein they reside.

If that were the entire Fourteenth Amendment, the future history of this country might have been very different. But the framers of the amendment went on to add:

> No State shall make or enforce any law which shall abridge the privileges or immunities of citizens of the United States, nor shall any State deprive any person of life, liberty, or property, without due process of law; nor deny to any person within its jurisdiction the equal protection of the laws.

Several phrases from this sentence—most notably, "privileges or immunities" and "due process" and "equal protection"—would have more effect on the way the nation developed than perhaps any other words in the entire Constitution. As a result, whole books have been written about the Fourteenth Amendment, and constitutional experts still do not agree on many points concerning it. While some of the long-range results will be discussed later, the reason why the Radical Republicans insisted on its adoption must be examined more closely right now.

In a word, politics lay behind the famous Fourteenth. Its underlying aim was to secure "perpetual ascendancy" for the Republican party, Thaddeus Stevens himself admitted—when he still felt confident of gaining inclusion of another clause, specifically granting former slaves the right to vote. Of course, it was widely assumed that the new voters would show their gratitude by voting solidly Republican.

A year after Stevens's death, this most radical of all the Radical Republican reforms was finally achieved in 1870, with the ratifying of the Fifteenth Amendment stating:

> The rights of citizens of the United States to vote shall not be denied or abridged by the United States or by any State on account of race, color, or previous condition of servitude.

If only human beings and the world they have made were more nearly perfect, this clause that seemingly completed the uplifting of the nation's blacks into full legal equality should have assured a high place among the heroes of America for Charles Sumner and Thaddeus Stevens. Instead, they have been almost forgotten because it would take another hundred years until the fine words they schemed to put into the Constitution acquired real meaning.

They are remembered mainly as schemers with good reason, for it seems undeniable that cold, political calculating mainly inspired them—in particular, a calculation harking back to one of the major compromises at the Constitutional Convention in 1787. At that time, to smooth over the already apparent conflict between slave and free states the framers had agreed that, for the purpose of determining how many representatives in the lower house of Congress the Southern states should have, their slaves would be counted on the basis of "three-fifths of all other persons."

Even with only this proportional representation, the slave states had been able to exert what Northerners felt to be an undue influence in Washington. For many years before the Civil War, the solidly Democratic South had stymied many Northern aims, and the Radical Republicans could not bear the prospect of having a still larger number of former rebels opposing them with the return of peace.

Senator Charles Sumner of Massachusetts led the Radical Republican push in the upper house of Congress to pass the Thirteenth, Fourteenth, and Fifteenth Amendments after the Civil War. *Courtesy New York Public Library Picture Collection*

Abolishing slavery had been the burning cause that had created their own party. Would victory mean defeat, though, on every other goal? For as soon as the three-fifths counting of blacks ended, the slave states would immediately and automatically be entitled to a minimum of fifteen additional members in the House of Representatives. It was this frightening figure that lay behind the whole Radical Republican postwar policy of imposing outside control on the South.

Yet some authorities say that the way the new provisional governments of the seceded states acted toward their exslaves during the first months of peace justified the Sumner-Stevens refusal to let them remain in power. Several of them enacted so-called "Black Codes," subjecting Negroes to a variety of indignities quite similar to the *apartheid* laws that would stir so much unrest in South Africa a century afterward. There were the same sort of limits on permitted occupations and requirements for carrying passes when venturing beyond restricted areas.

Undoubtedly, the Black Codes were bad and should not have been allowed. But fair-minded historians say that a gradual process of education could have achieved more positive results than the imposition of military rule under the reconstruction plan the Radical Republicans succeeded in adopting. The use of force only intensified the determination of Southerners to cope in their own manner with the enormous difficulties presented by the presence of hundreds of thousands of former slaves who had no training that would help them earn a living independently.

Late in the 1870s, the North finally gave up trying to rule the South. Then the conquered region, seething with anger, proceeded to wipe away any Negro gains made during the reconstruction period. By law and unwritten edict, it began imposing white supremacy implacably.

But what about the high-sounding war amendments to the United States Constitution? Didn't these protect black rights and prevent white harrassment? Unhappily, the treatment of blacks from the late 1870s until a new civil rights movement began attaining success in the 1950s would make it obvious

Thaddeus Stevens, one of the leaders of the Radical Republicans responsible for "the war amendments." *Courtesy New York Public Library Picture Collection*

that words alone cannot guarantee justice. Even in a nation ruled by written laws, the way words are interpreted may vary to a great extent in different eras.

In the 1870s, a series of civil rights cases that sought to strike down discrimination against blacks did reach the Supreme Court, but the judgments there went against Negroes who had been denied admission to theaters or some other public place. According to these verdicts, the war amendments forbade only state action that deprived blacks of equal treatment in very limited areas, such as filing a lawsuit to enforce a contract. The court held that the private owners of theaters could not be deprived of their own right to decide who should or should not be admitted.

Even on the matter of voting, which was certainly subject to regulation by the states, many judges were sufficiently blinded by racial prejudice to share the prevailing view that the various devices used to keep blacks from casting ballots did not violate the Fifteenth Amendment. Among the subterfuge adopted, the most notorious was the so-called "grandfather clause," holding that no person could vote unless it could be proved that his grandfather before him had been eligible to do so.

Completing the effectual nullification of the war amendments, in 1896 the Supreme Court issued a ruling in the case that would go down in constitutional history as *Plessy v. Ferguson*. More commonly, this landmark decision would be known as the verdict that legalized "Jim Crow."

In the then-current slang, any separate facility that blacks were required to use bore the name of this mythical individual. It was a separate railway car on a train leaving New Orleans that became the focal point of the far-reaching test case started by a black man named Homer Plessy. After he bought his ticket, he took a seat in one of the ordinary coaches used by white travelers.

Plessy refused to comply with the conductor's request that he move into the Jim Crow car. This led to his arrest, his appearance before a local judge named Ferguson—and eventually, an opinion by the Supreme Court containing a statement that in effect condemned blacks to second-class citizenship.

Speaking for the majority of his brethren, Justice Henry Billings Brown of Michigan upheld the doctrine that "separate but equal" facilities were neither unreasonable nor illegal. The framers of the Fourteenth Amendment, he declared, "could not have intended to abolish distinctions based upon color, or to enforce social, as distinguished from political, equality."

With "separate but equal" thereby established beyond question, segregated schools and segregated facilities of every sort would be sad evidence of the great distance between high principles and actual practice in the United States for many generations. At last, in 1954, *Plessy v. Ferguson* would be reversed, as a later chapter will relate.

Meanwhile, though, the Fourteenth Amendment was by no means forgotten. Quite the opposite happened, in fact, during the tremendous economic growth of the country following the Civil War. As big business gained increasing sway over American life, one after another of the states moved in one way or another to restrict or regulate the powers of corporations.

Then lawyers representing railroads or other industries being subjected to unwanted regulation made a great discovery. In the eyes of the law, corporations could be regarded as "persons." Eagerly, these lawyers seized on the Fourteenth Amendment's phrases forbidding state action that deprived "any person" of liberty or property and used them to win Supreme Court verdicts upholding corporate freedom from numerous kinds of restraints.

Some statistics compiled by a leading constitutional expert clearly show the importance of this amendment in the sphere of business. Until about 1880, fewer than a dozen cases involving interpretation of any of its clauses reached the Supreme Court. In the next twenty years, after lawyers for corporations began citing it to seek immunity from state regulations, there were more than 200 Fourteenth Amendment cases. Then around 1900, the rate doubled—and this flood has never ceased.

Yet the nature of the cases would change dramatically. Throughout the early decades of this century, the majority of the Supreme Court justices remained basically conservative. In case after case, they used the Fourteenth Amendment to strike down state laws aimed at protecting workers. Laws limiting working hours, for instance, were struck down on the grounds that any such measure constituted an unreasonable interference with the freedom of employers to run their own businesses.

A phrase borrowed from the French—*laissez faire*, which can be roughly translated "hands off!"—was adopted by the new science of economics to describe the prevailing philosophy about the proper governmental attitude toward business. Despite waves of opposition from time to time, laissez faire remained the guiding principle in American economic life decade after decade.

Then, in the 1930s, President Franklin Roosevelt found his New Deal program stymied by "nine old men" on the nation's highest court. When one after another of his major reforms was declared unconstitutional, the Supreme Court itself turned into a major issue, and this drama will be described in a later chapter. Here, though, it must be noted that the importance of the Fourteenth Amendment did not diminish. Finally, during the stirring civil rights revolution that started in the 1950s, this most versatile of amendments began serving the high purpose envisioned by the most high-minded of its sponsors.

9

Income Tax — and Senators

"IN THIS WORLD," Benjamin Franklin once wrote, "nothing is certain but death and taxes." Yet his oft-quoted quip could not have been referring to that most burdensome of imposts—the personal income tax—because it did not even exist during his century.

The first American income tax did not take effect until the Civil War. Then, under the stress of emergency, the new levy caused comparatively little controversy. With the coming of peace, though, this "golden egg" hatched by President Lincoln's Secretary of the Treasury turned into a major political issue that agitated the country repeatedly over the next several decades.

Above all, the argument in the late 1800s hinged on the basic question of whether the Constitution allowed the federal government to impose any such tax. Eventually, it would require the Sixteenth Amendment to settle the legality of the income tax indisputably. How that happened makes later debates about who should pay, and to what extent, seem rather calm.

But even if the discovery that a tax on the earnings of individual citizens can yield a lot of money is quite recent, experts trace the idea behind the income tax to primitive societies where tribal chiefs were supported by compulsory payments of grain or cattle. In exchange, the chief was supposed to see to it that his followers were defended against any marauding enemies.

But it was the Industrial Revolution, changing society so that money rather than grain or cattle became the medium of payment, that really laid the foundation for the modern income tax. The first example of a tax on income occurred in Great Britain, in 1799, during the nation's series of conflicts with France known as the Napoleonic Wars. Urgently needing funds to meet the costs of this continuing struggle, the British government adopted a 10 percent tax on the earnings of its citizenry.

In the young United States, the whole matter of the ways and means by which the new federal government should raise funds to support itself was particularly sensitive. Hadn't the hated British tax on tea helped to bring on the American Revolution? Not surprisingly, therefore, the founding fathers were very hesitant about imposing any taxes.

To start with, under the Articles of Confederation, the Congress that comprised the entire national governing apparatus could levy no taxes at all. It was obliged to beg contributions from the several states, like a poor relation. In fact, this total lack of financial power was one of the main reasons why the Articles of Confederation failed.

The lack was remedied in Article I, Section 8, of the Constitution: "The Congress shall have power to lay and collect taxes. . . ." But up until the Civil War, sales of land in the

West and import duties on goods from foreign countries provided the bulk of the federal revenue. The only domestic tax of any significance was an excise paid by distillers of whiskey—and even that almost provoked serious trouble when the so-called Whiskey Rebellion erupted in the backwoods of western Pennsylvania soon after George Washington became the nation's first President.

Briefly, during the War of 1812, President Madison's Secretary of the Treasury, a Philadelphia lawyer named Alexander P. Dallas, had talked about imposing an income tax to help pay the cost of the fighting. If he had been sane when he accepted the thankless task of financing this conflict, he grumbled, "it is not impossible that I shall go mad before I go away." Still, his desperate idea regarding a levy on incomes remained just an idea, and Dallas managed to raise enough money by the more acceptable policy of borrowing.

Fifty years later, though, the nation faced a far more serious crisis. In April of 1861, immediately following the firing on Fort Sumter by the newly-formed Southern Confederacy, President Lincoln called for the enlistment of 75,000 volunteers to put down the rebellion. His Secretary of the Treasury, Salmon P. Chase, shared the common belief in the North that the South would swiftly be defeated.

Yet a quick series of battles practically on the outskirts of Washington proved intensely sobering to Chase and many other Northern optimists. These Southern victories impelled him to include an unprecedented provision in the new revenue law he submitted to Congress during the summer of 1861. Till then, he had expected to finance the fighting merely by borrowing and by issuing "greenbacks"—new paper money designated as Treasury notes, though they could not be exchanged for gold and so their value was bound to diminish.

But the signs that the war was going to last much longer than he had anticipated made Treasury Secretary Chase call for many new taxes on items ranging from railway tickets to pianos. "Everything is taxed except coffins!" one writer exclaimed about the proposed revenue measure. Amid its dozens of clauses, the bill also authorized the nation's first tax on personal income.

Congressman Justin Morrill of Vermont was then the chairman of the House Ways and Means Committee's subcommittee on taxation. Tall and lean, with the canny blue eyes of a successful Yankee storeowner, he spoke up frankly to his colleagues. This income tax was "one of the least defensible" of the proposals on the long list the Secretary of the Treasury had presented, he said. But considering the war emergency, he advised approving it anyway, and his advice was taken.

So, in 1862, families all over the Union began receiving visits from Treasury agents who handed them a four-page form headed "Internal Revenue—Income Tax." It contained a series of questions concerning ownership of real estate and possessions like silverware or even yachts, besides inquiring: "What was your income last year?"

On the basis of the answers provided, householders were required to pay a tax of 3 percent of any income over $600, rising to 5 percent on income above $10,000, with various deductions permitted in calculating the amount due.

Thus, right from the outset, the income tax applied a higher rate to the earnings of the rich—a fact that most people considered fair, for the less well-to-do needed to spend a greater proportion of their earnings on food, clothing, and shelter than the wealthy did. It could hardly be expected, however, that prosperous citizens would see the matter the same way.

The most vehement objections to the new tax revolved, though, around one feature of the collection procedure. As a means for ensuring compliance, revenue agents were supposed to allow public inspection of everybody's tax statements. Therefore, lists publicizing who had just paid, and how much, soon were being printed by newspapers.

Then Congressman Morrill noted wryly that Americans were just like people everywhere else—"not averse to a knowledge of the secrets of others, though quite unwilling to disclose their own." Yet the publicity continued, prodding patriotic citizens of the North to keep on paying the emergency levy year after year.

In the South, no income tax ever was adopted, at least partly because it could not have yielded much in that predominantly agricultural region. In the manufacturing North, the levy on earnings turned out to be such a boon to the hard-pressed Treasury that even when the war ended in 1865 the tax did not. During 1866, it brought in nearly 25 percent of the total federal revenue.

To give up this golden stream was not easy. Despite mounting clamor, which stopped the publicizing of individual payments but increased concern about cheating, it was not till 1872 that Congress finally completed a gradual phasing-out of the wartime measure taxing the earnings of the nation's citizenry.

Far from dying away, though, the issue kept stirring new sparks of controversy. Over the next two decades—remarkable as it may seem—proposals for making the income tax a permanent feature of American life acquired strong support among a large portion of the population.

In this period when big business was becoming the most powerful force affecting the nation's economy, conflicts of many sorts developed between the "haves" and the "have-nots." The increasing influence exerted by New York's Wall Street aroused increasing protest among the workers and farmers of the West and South. To the less prosperous, it appeared only common sense that the rich should be taxed more heavily than anybody else—a notion denounced by one Republican Senator as "socialism, communism, devilism."

Actually, the focal point of the economic debate was the Republican policy of protecting American industries from foreign competition by charging a high tariff on imports of goods that had been produced abroad. During the solidly Republican 1870s, these duties on imports served the additional purpose of providing the main source of revenue for the federal government. Unfortunately, though, the high import duties also assured that the prices American consumers paid for shoes or other necessities were substantially above what such items would have cost in a free market.

By the early 1890s, an upstart political movement out in the hinterlands was pressing hard for lower tariffs—and an income tax. Unable to win the White House, the Populists still achieved the sort of indirect success that other third parties have scored throughout American history. In effect, the most widely appealing planks in its platform were borrowed by one of the two major parties, in this case the Democrats.

So the election of the Democratic President Grover Cleveland in 1892 brought an intense new campaign to reduce tariffs at least slightly, and to restore the income tax. By then, the Republican opposition had seized on one compelling argument against any such levy: that it could not legally be imposed because the Constitution did not permit it.

Even some Democrats agreed. Still, a leading authority not only saw nothing wrong with the income tax, he actually praised it. Simeon Baldwin, a recent president of the American Bar Association, said of the income tax: "It is one of the fairest measures that can be devised to fill up the Treasury, without burdening the people at large. . . . It throws its burden on those who can bear it best." And Congress, now having a Democratic majority, was convinced.

Thus, the second federal income tax took effect on January 1, 1895, providing for a 2 percent levy on all income over $4,000. Given the high exemption, it affected only a small part of the population, mainly in cities along the Atlantic seaboard.

But the Republicans, fearing that higher rates would surely be adopted soon if the unpropertied masses were allowed to set this dangerous precedent, immediately swung into action. Throughout the Civil War period, not a single test case had been filed challenging the constitutionality of the first federal income tax. Belatedly, in 1881, a case harking back to the wartime levy had reached the Supreme Court, which had unanimously upheld the tax. However, the forces opposing the new levy felt confident that a stronger case could now be made and set out to do so.

A Massachusetts man named Charles Pollock became the person who would go down in the annals of the Supreme Court as the instigator of the important proceeding known as *Pollock v. Farmers Loan and Trust Company*. But the case is remembered mainly because of the extremely clever lawyer Pollock hired. His name was Joseph H. Choate.

Sixty-three years old in 1895, Choate had reached the peak of his profession by adding wit and sarcasm to his courtroom defenses of the corporations he usually represented. With a distinguished air, as befitted a man repeatedly selected to head groups of New York civic leaders ranging from the Harvard College Alumni to the trustees of the American Museum of Natural History, he also possessed a voice of great resonance.

Addressing the Supreme Court on the subject of the income tax, Choate treated the justices as if they all were members of the same club. He stood at ease, with one hand in his trousers pocket, explaining that right-thinking Americans must stop the "communistic march" that would be inevitable, should this tax be upheld. He warned that the passage of a 2 percent income tax could not but lead to a 20 percent tax, unless the nation's highest court outlawed such a frightening example of the poor coercing the rich through control over Congress.

While delivering this emotional appeal, Choate was shrewd enough to tie it in with a solemn legal argument. He claimed he was basing his case on two clauses in the Constitution's Article I that set forth the powers of Congress. The first of these specified that any direct tax "shall be uniform throughout the United States," and the other prescribed that "No . . . direct tax shall be laid unless in proportion" to the population of each state.

But this argument violated simple common sense because the growth of cities and factory towns since 1800 had produced a very unequal pattern of population that could not have been foreseen when the Constitution was written. Thus, to apply an income tax on the basis of current census figures would mean that a poor sharecropper in North Carolina would owe four times as much as any New York taxpayer. Clearly, such inequality was forbidden by the clause about uniformity.

So the real question before the Court was whether the income tax must be considered a direct tax as the term had been understood by the framers of the Constitution. Yet how could they possibly have meant to describe an income tax this way in 1787? For no such method of raising revenue had yet been invented.

No matter, though, that constitutional experts over the years since 1895 have shaken their heads over Choate's performance, it swayed the majority of the Supreme Court in his day. Chief Justice Melville W. Fuller, a pompous man from Maine with a flowing moustache and a grave distrust of reformist tendencies, himself wrote the five-to-four decision declaring the income tax unconstitutional.

This opinion struck some Republicans in 1895 as comparable with the famous verdicts of Chief Justice John Marshall that had first established the Supreme Court's right to be the final arbiter in interpreting the Constitution. But other reactions were much less complimentary. "The overthrow of the income tax . . . is another victory of greed over need," the New York *World* asserted.

Future writers would be even more outspoken. "It was one of the unhappiest decisions in the history of the Court," Professor Allan Nevins told the readers of his biography of President Cleveland in the 1930s. Another leading historian added: "The income tax decision unquestionably excited more feeling than any action by the Supreme Court since the Dred Scott opinion."

Still, the outlawing of the income tax by no means made it a dead issue. The same forces that had revived it after the Civil War kept it very much alive in the early years of the twentieth century. However, its supporters faced the daunting prospect of somehow having to push through a new amendment to the Constitution specifically authorizing this form of taxation.

Ever since the flurry of Negro rights amendments soon after the surrender of the Southern Confederacy, the complicated process required to adopt any further amendments had been defeating groups of reformers, most notably those working to grant women the vote and to prohibit alcoholic beverages. But the dedicated members of such groups were almost always political outsiders. In the case of the income tax, some very experienced insiders became involved, speeding up the process. Even so, adoption of the Sixteenth Amendment took nearly twenty years.

The first sign that the issue had entered the political mainstream came in 1906 when President Theodore Roosevelt sent a message to Congress, expressing his personal feeling that the country ought to have an income tax. "The man of great wealth owes a peculiar obligation to the state," Roosevelt said, "because he derives special advantages from the mere existence of government."

This Republican chief executive, who was a wealthy man himself, had already caused much distress to the conservatives in his party by his outbursts of "progressive" ideas. Possibly because he did not wish to antagonize too many old-line supporters, he did not follow through on his income tax advocacy. By one of the great ironies of American politics, it was Roosevelt's successor—the much more conservative William Howard Taft—who, in 1909, was all but forced into urging Congressional approval of the following amendment:

> The Congress shall have power to lay and collect taxes on incomes, from whatever source derived, without apportionment among the several States, and without regard to any census or enumeration.

Part of the reason for Taft's support was an alarming Treasury deficit. Also, progress-minded Republicans had been joining their Democratic colleagues in opposing continued high tariffs. And even in the Senate, much less radical than

the House of Representatives, there appeared to be sufficient votes for an alternate plan Taft found less appealing,
the passage of a third federal income tax measure.

No matter that it was just fourteen years since the Supreme Court had outlawed the second tax. By now, the temper of the country, and of the nation's highest court, had
changed enough to make a reversal of the 1895 decision
more than likely. Taft, who would end his career as an esteemed Chief Justice himself, thought any such reversal
would lower the Supreme Court's prestige. As the lesser
evil, he urged that both houses of Congress enact a resolution endorsing the proposed Sixteenth Amendment. Then it
would be up to the legislatures of the several states to vote
yes or no on the income tax.

Undoubtedly, Taft felt in 1909 that it would take a long
time until the required thirty-six states ratified the amendment. Perhaps it would never pass, but at least its supporters might be more tractable after having had their way in
Congress.

And yet reform was in the air. By 1912, the year of another presidential election, the platforms of both major parties favored the income tax amendment. Then, on February
5, 1913, Wyoming became the thirty-sixth state to send notice of its ratification to Washington.

So Woodrow Wilson, the new Democratic President, increased his own reputation as a great reformer almost acci-
dentally. It just happened to be during his first year in the
White House that the first indisputably legal federal income
tax was enacted by Congress. From then on, this levy would
keep on providing more and more federal revenue—over
$380 billion annually by 1985, constituting about 37 percent
of the federal budget.

Of course, specific provisions of the income tax continued

to arouse controversy. More than seventy years after the amendment, a major effort to "reform" the tax law created one of the major issues during Ronald Reagan's presidency in the 1980s. Yet there had long since ceased to be any question about whether Americans should pay some form of tax on their earnings because that had already been irrevocably decided back in 1913.

Of less personal impact on every citizen, another constitutional amendment was adopted almost simultaneously with the one authorizing the income tax. It was the Seventeenth Amendment, stating that United States Senators shall be elected by direct popular vote, instead of being chosen by the legislatures of the states as the Constitution had originally required.

It was no coincidence that direct election of the members of the Senate became the law of the land in May of 1913, only three months after the income tax amendment. The two issues had become closely related during the intense politicking preceding action on either one of them. For the die-hard conservatism of some Senators accountable only to their state legislatures had aroused much anguish among reformers striving toward a fairer system of federal taxation.

Traditionally, the Senate had always been slower and more deliberate about passing laws than the House of Representatives. That was as the founding fathers had wished when they gave Senators six-year terms, instead of just the two years for members of the lower house, and specified that Senators were to be chosen on a more elite basis—by the presumably more solid citizens elected to state legislatures, rather than by the entire electorate.

But what the founding fathers had not envisioned was the rise of powerful special interests after the Civil War. Railroads and other major industries found it not too difficult to "buy" United States Senators, just by making sure that the comparatively few members of any state legislature chose a Senator friendly to the industry's interests.

As a result, toward the end of the 1800s, certain members of the Senate in Washington were clearly identified by those in the know as "the Senator from Steel" or "the Senator from Sugar." That latter personage, a deaf old man supposedly representing Louisiana, showed the extent to which the system had been abused when he approached the Senate's Republican leader one day and shouted, "If I don't vote right, you'll understand it's because I don't hear what it is you want."

Since support of high tariffs had been one of the main motivating impulses in the "buying" of Senators, it was the increasingly unpopular stand these Senators took on tariff questions that stirred increasing public discontent. Then the push for an income tax during the same period opened the way for senatorial reform, too.

So it happened that, in 1912, both houses of Congress responded to this public pressure by approving a resolution favoring an amendment providing for direct election of members of the Senate. Then there was quite a speedy response by the legislatures of the several states. Only one year later, in May of 1913, word reached Washington that affirmative action had already been taken by thirty-six states—and the Seventeenth Amendment was officially declared part of the law of the land.

10

The Noble Experiment

. . . the manufacture, sale, or transportation of intox-
icating liquors . . . is hereby prohibited.

WITH THOSE CRUCIAL WORDS in the Eighteenth Amendment to the Constitution, the United States entered one of
the strangest periods any country has ever experienced.
While President Herbert Hoover called Prohibition "an experiment noble in motive and far-reaching in purpose," it
created such a giddy surge of lawlessness during the 1920s
that after just fourteen years another amendment brought its
repeal.

But short as this national test turned out to be, the pressures leading toward it had been growing for a long time,
starting even before the thirteen American colonies declared
their independence. In Philadelphia, early in the 1770s, a
devout Quaker had stood up at a prayer meeting to express
the first recorded concern about other people's drinking. He
was, he said, "oppress'd with the smell of rum from the
breaths of those who sat around him."

Two centuries later, the mere idea of a sedate religious

gathering being bothered by an alcoholic aroma may seem surprising. Yet historians report that the original English and Dutch settlers in the New World probably carried kegs of spirits with them, then kept on importing or distilling astonishing quantities by today's standards. Hardly anybody thought drinking was sinful then; in fact, many considered it almost a necessity.

At the breakfast tables of highly respectable families, a hot toddy of rum and boiling water sweetened with a little molasses routinely warmed the men, and a few spoonfuls of the mixture often were fed to the children. When heavy work had to be done, some extra fortifying was taken for granted. Inevitably, a certain amount of drunkenness resulted.

Yet the idea that Americans ought to aim for perfection had already taken root. It was this attitude, insisting there must be a way to solve every sort of problem, that would turn the drinking habits of individual citizens into a major public issue. The process really started with the printing of an earnest pamphlet, written by another Quaker in 1774.

The Mighty Destroyer Displayed was just the top line of its title, which went on to promise "Some Account of the Dreadful Havock made by the mistaken Use as well as Abuse of Distilled Spirituous Liquors." In effect, this marked the opening of a 150-year campaign that would increasingly agitate the nation until Prohibition was tried.

By the 1780s, the cause had already received medical endorsement from Dr. Benjamin Rush of Philadelphia, a well-known patriot who had been a signer of the Declaration of Independence. At least in the scope of his interests, he somewhat resembled his friend Benjamin Franklin, although the latter genially served the best imported beer when he entertained his fellow delegates at the Constitutional Convention in 1787.

But even if Dr. Rush enjoyed fine wines himself, he became something like the founding father of the temperance movement when he wrote *An Inquiry into the Effect of Ardent Spirits*. Along with some sound warnings about overindulgence, he presented such a horrendous list of ailments—from epilepsy to madness—allegedly caused by drink that his *Inquiry* captured wide attention. It was credited with inspiring the start of a number of local groups dedicated to encouraging personal vows against any further imbibing.

Then around 1810 a dynamic preacher named Lyman Beecher provided the impetus for a much more ambitious drive. Attending a conference of Connecticut ministers, he was so appalled by the "grogshop" atmosphere at the meeting that he composed a series of sermons on the evils of drink.

"Much is said about the prudent use of spirits," the Reverend Dr. Beecher thundered, "but we might as well speak of the prudent use of the plague—of fire handled prudently around powder—of poison taken prudently every day." These fervent words, printed and spread around the country, gave the signal that other high-minded Americans quickly heeded.

Soon there were hundreds of new associations working to promote the cause they called temperance. In 1833, about 5,000 local societies from every point of the compass sent delegates to a national convention in Philadelphia, where they formed the American Temperance Union. Its main project was circulating personal pledges against drinking— pledges signed by countless individuals, including a young Illinois lawyer named Abraham Lincoln who had no trouble at all with alcohol.

According to any dictionary, the principal meaning of the

word "temperance" is "habitual moderation." Yet the severely moral leaders of the temperance movement quite agreed with Lyman Beecher about the dangers of even moderate drinking. What they were striving for was actually total abstinence, at first on a voluntary basis. Within just a few years, however, they moved to make giving up drink compulsory.

Largely because of a spellbinding crusader named Neal Dow, the state of Maine became the scene of the first statewide test of a prohibition statute. In 1846, Dow convinced the Maine legislature to pass a law banning alcoholic beverages, except for medicinal purposes. News of this stirred great excitement among temperance groups elsewhere, and they pushed the legislatures of several other states to pass their own versions of "the Maine law."

Meanwhile, Maine itself swiftly proved how very difficult it is to legislate morality. All kinds of devious ways for selling drinks developed practically overnight, at least some of them adding new words to the language. "Bootleggers" were persons who carried bottles in the wide tops of their boots to dark alleys where money and liquor could be exchanged safely. "Blind pig" became common slang for any place that dispensed drinks illegally, after some ingenious dealers set up tents in which they claimed they were merely exhibiting an afflicted animal—and the people who paid the required admission charge were served only "free" drinks.

Faced with such widespread disdain for the law, Maine set another precedent by repealing it. Still, the spellbinding Dow went lecturing around the country and collected scores of medals or other trophies from temperance admirers. If the experience in other states also followed Maine's example, there were certainly some positive results from this initial flurry of anti-drunkenness agitation.

Public awareness about the dangers of excessive drinking did reduce consumption to quite an extent. Also, the idea of "local option," whereby drinking establishments could be regulated or even banned in accord with the wishes of local citizens, spread widely. Then came the Civil War, halting most efforts on peacetime concerns like temperance.

After the fighting ended, there was a tremendous burst of anti-drinking activism by a great new reformist force the war had unleashed. Especially in the North, women who had previously accepted the prevailing outlook limiting them to home and family interests had discovered hidden talents. Holding fairs or other events to raise money for hospials, they learned how capable they could be at promoting causes in the outside world.

Temperance, for some very good reasons, was a cause particularly appealing to females. Except for an occasional glass of wine or various sweet "cordials," such as blackberry brandy, few respectable women did any drinking themselves—at least openly. There was, though, a certain amount of secret tippling, and it would later become known that some of the most popular medicinal "tonics" taken by the most high-minded ladies really contained about 20 percent alcohol.

But it was drinking by men that spurred the women reformers. No matter that only a small minority of husbands became hopeless drunkards, the plight of any wife tied to such a man was terribly sad because the laws of the day gave her no help at all. Divorce was difficult and much frowned-upon—and, if she had children, their father could legally keep them himself.

As a result, wives were all but forced to suffer many sorts of abuse from husbands who drank too much. And poor children might actually go hungry unless they took part in a real-life version of a scene out of the famous temperance drama, "Ten Nights in a Bar Room," staged by traveling companies that brought it to the smallest towns. Its big moment at each performance came when "Little Mary" sang piteously: "Father, Dear Father, Come Home With Me Now!" Wiping aside their tears, women in every audience yearned "to *do* something" about liquor.

By 1874, thousands of religious wives and sisters had therefore joined in founding the Woman's Christian Temperance Union, soon known everywhere as the WCTU. Its goal, like that of earlier temperance associations, began by being merely to educate the citizenry regarding the dangers of drink.

It helped a lot to publicize their cause when the wife of President Rutherford B. Hayes, inaugurated in 1877, made headlines by refusing to serve any wine in the White House. "Lemonade Lucy," the newspapers called her. But the cause was helped far more momentously when a strong-willed educator named Frances Elizabeth Willard decided to enlist.

Growing up on a Wisconsin farm, she had been a red-haired tomboy who insisted on having her friends call her "Frank." Thirty-five years old when she was elected corresponding secretary of the new WCTU, she had already become a leading figure in the Illinois town of Evanston, near Chicago. Miss Willard had moved there to preside over the Evanston College for Ladies, closely linked with Northwestern University. After her separate branch was absorbed by Northwestern, she had stayed on as dean of women.

Yet she craved a more exciting role. To her, it seemed obvious that the WCTU ought to exert a strong influence politically, but its original president rejected Miss Willard's plan for supporting Miss Susan B. Anthony's votes-for-women drive as the best means of advancing the temperance cause. "We do not propose to trail our skirts through the mire of politics," this lady pronounced.

Just four years later, Frances Willard won the WCTU presidency herself. While most of its members still felt that Miss Anthony's suffrage campaign was too radical, they enormously admired their own leader's energy and enthusiasm. During the next twenty years, she used vast amounts of both qualities in making the WCTU a very visible presence on the American scene.

Solemnly, it held prayer meetings on the sidewalks outside thousands of saloons where strong drink was being consumed. It sponsored teaching programs in the nation's schools, striving to convince boys and girls to sign pledges against ever tasting beer or wine or whiskey by showing them fearsome demonstrations. For instance, a beaker of alcohol would be poured over the white of an egg, which immediately hardened—and didn't that prove a similar hardening would happen to any drinker's stomach? More cheerfully, in flower-decked halls, speakers at the WCTU's annual conventions kept offering progress reports about the passage of local "dry laws" in an increasing number of counties.

Adoption of statewide restrictions in one state after another was what they were all working toward. Even to Miss Willard, the sometimes-mentioned notion of pushing through an amendment to the United States Constitution prohibiting liquor everywhere seemed farfetched. The process was very cumbersome and, apart from the three Negro rights amendments soon after the Civil War, no proposals for new amendments had been seriously considered since the early days of the Republic.

Still, Miss Willard herself gave the country a bit of light-hearted evidence of her underlying goal. When someone presented her with a new collie pup, she named him "Pro-hibition"—"Hibbie" for short. At least to this extent, the WCTU did become openly committed to the aim of national prohibition, but its conservative membership kept shying away from outright political maneuvering.

In 1898, Miss Willard died of a blood disease. While mil-lions of women remained deeply loyal to her cause, the WCTU's influence was concentrated in the towns and smaller cities of the Middle West. It appeared possible that the move-ment might subside into merely a local phenomenon.

Then just a year later, from the Kansas village of Medicine Lodge near the border of the Oklahoma Territory, came star-tling news that put temperance on front pages again. An-other strong-willed woman had begun storming into local saloons and personally smashing bottles by the hundreds, besides shattering barroom mirrors. Her name was Carrie Nation.

"Men!" she would cry out as she entered each establish-ment. "I have come to save you from a drunkard's fate." She then proceeded, while loudly singing one of her favorite hymns, to break so much glass that rivers of "booze" ran out into the streets.

Throughout American history, there has never been a more peculiar character than this self-appointed destroyer. Serious mental instability marked her whole family—her mother had spent many years telling people she was Queen Victoria of England, before being confined in a hospital. But crazy as Carrie Nation herself seemed to many people, she still stirred a powerful new wave of support for prohibiting all sale of liquor.

Nearly six feet tall, wearing a black bonnet and a long black dress, she made it easy for cartoonists to picture her as a fierce, avenging angel doing battle against "the Demon

A cartoonist ridiculed both sides in the campaign preceding adoption of the Prohibition amendment, showing Carrie Nation with her hatchet, spouting Biblical quotes against drinking, while a bartender cites passages in the Bible defending his calling. *Courtesy New York Public Library Picture Collection*

Rum." Her choice of weapon further simplified the task of dramatizing her. At first, she used ordinary stones or bricks to do her smashing, but soon she tried a sledgehammer, and then she discovered the tool that suited her best—a sharp-bladed little hatchet.

Within a few months, Mrs. Nation and her hatchet had become internationally famous. Cannily, she began selling miniature hatchets to souvenir-collectors for a dime or a quarter, earning enough to pay her expenses as she traveled around Kansas. Yet there was a core of reason beneath her bizarre antics, making her an authentic heroine, at least for a brief period, among dedicated temperance advocates.

As she kept telling interviewers, her first husband had

showed up drunk at their wedding and, after only six months, died a horrible drunkard's death. Then the pain she endured lay buried until, finally, the awful sight of saloons openly selling their poison in Medicine Lodge had impelled her to start her smashing.

Yet Carrie Nation's home state of Kansas was supposedly "dry." In 1880, it had become the first state to adopt a prohibition amendment to its state constitution. Although various other states had previously passed laws banning liquor, repealing mere laws had turned out to be not very difficult, and so the temperance movement had put its faith in the less easily reversible procedure of amending the basic charter of each state.

But the Kansas amendment had by no means ended liquor sales there. Soon most towns had more saloons than ever, and because they were operating illegally they became increasingly sordid hangouts where all sorts of crimes were hatched. It was this embarrassing situation that kept the authorities from holding Mrs. Nation in jail after she began her smashing.

Although she was arrested repeatedly, prosecutors could not find any solid grounds for trying her in court. Eventually, her own grandiose delusions relieved them of the necessity for dealing with her. She let promoters take advantage of her notoriety by advertising a lecture tour— and soon she was being hooted at by audiences at the lowest kinds of freak shows.

Still, Mrs. Nation's few years of smashing had a lasting impact. The publicity she gained for the cause of temperance certainly helped another new organization to undertake a coldly practical campaign aimed at swaying the nation's lawmakers. It was the Anti-Saloon League, which finally made the cause catch fire.

Political-minded men had begun trying to do this as early as 1869, when a group calling itself the Prohibition Party was formed in Chicago. From the presidential election of 1872 onward, it put up its own candidate for the White House every four years—one or another dedicated reformer, among them "the father of the Maine Law," Neal Dow.

The first Prohibition nominee, in 1872, received only 5,608 votes. By 1900, a man named John G. Woolley had increased the Prohibitionist tally to nearly 209,000, but in that election the Republican William McKinley won with over seven million votes and the Democratic second-runner received more than six million. Clearly, the Prohibitionists were a long way from victory.

In Ohio, however, two intense men embarked on plans for accomplishing the same sort of political magic that other third parties had previously used to gain their own objectives. What they had in mind was to force one or even both of the major parties to endorse their own aim of banning strong drink throughout the nation.

The elder of these Ohioans was a Congregationalist minister named Howard Hyde Russell. A compelling speaker, he often told audiences about how he had hated passing any saloon, until one day he was moved to send up a prayer: "O God, stop this!" And then, he related: "God plainly said to me, 'You know how to do it. Go and help answer your own prayers!'"

So the Reverend Mr. Russell started the Ohio Anti-Saloon League—"the nucleus of the most ruthless good-cause lobby the United States ever saw," in the words of one historian. But nothing else Russell did had more effect than his recruitment of a student orator he encountered in 1893 at a prohibition meeting on the campus of Oberlin College.

Wayne Bidwell Wheeler, from a not-very-prosperous farm

family, was a junior working his way through school waiting on tables and serving as a janitor. Still, he managed to find time for practicing public speaking, and his favorite topic was the evils of drink because a drunken neighbor had once attacked him with a pitchfork.

Besides being very ambitious, young Wheeler possessed a positive sense that his own side was the right side in any debate. He so impressed the Reverend Mr. Russell that a job was offered to him. After he went to work for the Anti-Saloon League, Wheeler himself decided he would be more useful if he had a law degree and, studying at night, he earned it in 1898.

To sum up Wheeler's vast contribution to the Prohibition cause is not easy, because much of his activity was rather devious. Beyond prosecuting more than 2,000 cases involving violations of local dry laws, he showed his skill at political maneuvering by seeing to it that a popular Republican governor was defeated when he held back from wholeheartedly supporting a local-option measure.

Among Wheeler's tactics was sending women pickets to march outside of polling places, carrying emotional signs about the horrors of drink. He also arranged for children to plead with each arriving voter: "Mister, for God's sake, don't vote for whiskey!" Owing to Wheeler's great success in Ohio, he went on to become general counsel of the Anti-Saloon League of America in Washington.

"The Saloon Must Go!" That was the slogan Wheeler hammered away at in the nation's capital. And, by 1916, his efforts to make sure that only friends of his cause were elected to Congress all but guaranteed that an amendment to the Constitution prohibiting liquor all over the country would soon be recommended by both the Senate and the House of Representatives.

Even though a majority of ordinary citizens was far from convinced that all drinking should be forbidden, in the South and the Middle West, the strongholds of anti-drinking sentiment, the cause was undeniably popular. And "Wets" elsewhere were no match for "Wheelerism," as unfriendly writers described the Anti-Saloon League's hard-hitting policies.

So, on December 18, 1917, Congress took the last step required before the proposed Eighteenth Amendment went out to the several states to be either ratified or rejected. Thirty-six state legislatures would have to approve it if it were to become the law of the land.

Again Wheeler swung into action, and he was assisted by a powerful combination of other factors. In Europe, the great conflict that would go down in history as the First World War had started three years earlier. Despite President Wilson's attempts to keep the United States neutral, the threat to American ships from German submarines had made him ask Congress in April 1917 to join England and France in fighting Germany.

With the nation at war, the argument that Prohibition would help us win was advanced by leaders in many industries. They claimed that if factory workers could not drink over weekends, there would be less absenteeism on Mondays and more weapons would be produced. Amid the patriotic emotion prevailing, this idea bolstered all the other moral and medical and political points in favor of the amendment with which Wheeler bombarded the members of state legislatures.

No doubt, his political skills had the most effect. By then, Wheeler's ways of defeating lawmakers suspected of "Wet" tendencies could usually bring any waverers into the "Dry" camp. Thus it happened that, on January 16, 1919, the ratification of the Eighteenth Amendment was completed.

But the amendment itself specified a year's delay, from the date of its approval, until Prohibition would actually become the law of the land. This was to allow the winding down of the whole machinery for making and selling liquor in an orderly manner. Yet that did not happen.

Under the barrage of propaganda favoring Prohibition, most lawmakers had seemingly overlooked an important fact. Apart from "Bible belt" areas, the majority of Americans saw nothing wrong with occasional drinking. While about 5 percent of those who drank might do so excessively, causing some serious problems, the other 95 percent rarely caused any trouble to law enforcement authorities.

It quickly became apparent, though, that enforcing Prohibition would be all but impossible. Instead of closing their doors for good by January of 1920, when the amendment took effect, the owners of most saloons merely put curtains over them or drilled little peepholes in them. Any thirsty person could just knock, then murmur some phrase like "Joe sent me" to gain admittance. Inside these thousands of establishments, which became known as "speakeasies," liquor was often served in teacups rather than ordinary glasses, but huge amounts of it were certainly served.

Much of it had been smuggled across the borders from Canada or Mexico. Also, ships anchored safely offshore unloaded cases of bottles into speedy little launches that landed their cargo on beaches along every coastline. And in remote parts of the countryside, millions of additional gallons were illegally distilled.

There was no way that local police or federal agents could stem such an enormous tide. Despite flurries of raids, moreover, it soon became clear that most law enforcement bodies were not seriously trying to interfere with bootleggers—for a terrible epidemic of police corruption also accompanied Prohibition. In every city and town, it was an open secret that illegal liquor dealers were buying "protection" by "paying off" those supposedly enforcing the law.

Most seriously, the illegal liquor trade involved such immense profits that it made organized crime into a big business. Gangsters like Al Capone and Dutch Schultz ran their own empires harshly, using hired gunmen to murder their enemies, and there seemed no way to stop this orgy of crime.

No way except to repeal Prohibition. Throughout the 1920s, a gradually rising pressure for repeal developed, particularly in major cities. While most Republicans running for office were still unyielding "Drys," more and more Democrats openly proclaimed themselves to be "Wets."

By 1932, when the Democratic Franklin D. Roosevelt won the presidency, public opinion had turned decisively. On February 20, 1933, Congress proposed a new amendment—the Twenty-first—and urged prompt approval of it by the several states. The gist of the new proposal was:

The eighteenth article of amendment to the Constitution of the United States is hereby repealed.

On December 5, 1933, the roster of states that ratified the change reached the required number of thirty-six—and the "noble experiment" it had taken so long to adopt was ended after barely fourteen years of sad experience.

11

Remember the Ladies

ALL THE WAY BACK IN 1777, just a year after the Declaration of Independence, Abigail Adams had written to her husband John:

> In the new code of laws which I suppose it will be necessary for you to make, I desire you would remember the ladies and be more generous and favorable to them than your ancestors. Do not put such unlimited power into the hands of the husbands. Remember, all men would be tyrants if they could. If particular care and attention is not paid to the ladies, we are determined to foment a rebellion, and will not hold ourselves bound by any laws in which we have no voice or representation.

Still, the founding fathers of the United States simply ignored the fact that about half of the new nation's population was female. By doing so, they showed no special anti-feminist feeling. Throughout recorded history, the notion that women should have an active part in political life had rarely been taken seriously.

But the climate of equality in America eventually did foster the sort of "rebellion" about which Abigail Adams had playfully warned. It took a long time, though. The struggle that at last resulted in the Nineteenth Amendment to the Constitution—granting women the right to vote—did not even start until 1848.

That summer, a judge's daughter who might have become an exceptional lawyer herself, if it had been possible then for any female to secure the required training, called a meeting. Elizabeth Cady Stanton, the thirty-three-year-old mother of three lively little boys, lived in the peaceful village of Seneca Falls in upstate New York, quite an unlikely setting for any world-shaking gathering. Yet she insisted on going ahead because Lucretia Mott was visiting the area.

Eight years earlier and 3,000 miles away, Lizzie on her honeymoon had met the much-admired Mrs. Mott at a great conclave of anti-slavery reformers in London. While the strong-minded young bride—who had refused to marry unless the word "obey" was omitted from her wedding ceremony—had only accompanied her husband Henry, a noted speaker and writer for the abolitionist cause, Mrs. Mott was one of the handful of women named official delegates by some American anti-slavery societies. The arrival of these females much displeased the English hosts of the convention.

Lizzie Stanton never forgot her own outrage when the famous Mrs. Mott and the other women delegates were seated *behind a curtain*—so they could hear the proceedings but neither speak nor vote on any issue. "It's time," she sputtered to Mrs. Mott, "it's time some demand is made for new liberties for women." Mrs. Mott, a sedate Quaker twice as old as Lizzie, had nodded soberly, creating a warm bond between the two of them.

Even so, Lizzie Stanton's boldness eight years later made Mrs. Mott uneasy. Impulsively, Lizzie wrote a notice for the local newspaper announcing a two-day convention in a Seneca Falls church "to discuss the social, civil, and religious condition and rights of women." While there were surely many unfair laws and customs limiting women's lives, Mrs. Mott agreed, wouldn't it be wiser if they waited till they could hold their meeting in some large city where they might attract much more attention?

But Lizzie said she was fed up with merely collecting pickle recipes and trying to keep her boys out of mischief. She insisted that even in Seneca Falls, women by the dozen would come from miles around to see and hear the eminent Mrs. Mott.

Next, Lizzie read aloud the statement she had prepared as the focus for discussion at the meeting. After listing many restrictions, such as laws preventing married women from owning any property, this "Declaration of Sentiments" brashly asserted that women must be allowed to share "the inalienable right" to vote.

"Why, Lizzie," Mrs. Mott said, "thee will make us ridiculous!"

Mrs. Mott was right. For many years after the Seneca Falls convention of July 1848, the idea that women should be permitted to cast ballots was widely ridiculed. In the long run, however, Lizzie Stanton's daring would be amply vindicated. Her "Declaration of Sentiments," signed by sixty-eight women and thirty-two men, began a tremendous wave of change not only in the United States but all around the world.

Yet the campaign involved intense emotions, touching as it did on the basic matter of the relationship between men and women. That was why a change that might not seem very radical today took so long to accomplish. While the white-haired Mrs. Mott helped a lot at the outset, an amazingly efficient young teacher soon became Mrs. Stanton's partner in promoting the woman's rights movement. Her name was Susan Brownell Anthony.

Susan B., the Stanton children called her. During the 1850s, as the Stanton family grew to include five boys and two girls, time after time the tall, sturdy Susan B. would come striding toward their front door for another stay of several weeks. These extended visits served a variety of purposes. They gave the childless Miss Anthony, who had a much warmer nature than stiff portraits of her ever would indicate, a welcome taste of the joys of motherhood. And while she temporarily took over running the boisterous household, Mrs. Stanton sat at her desk reading, writing, planning.

For Susan always brought along stacks of petitions or other documents pertaining to the cause of woman's rights. Yet she lacked Mrs. Stanton's quick facility at setting strategy and writing speeches. As Henry Stanton wryly told his wife, "You stir up Susan, and she stirs up the world."

Five years younger than her married friend, Susan had been born on a farm near the Massachusetts town of Adams in 1820. During her childhood, her Quaker father had moved his wife and eight children to upper New York State. The second eldest in this high-minded family, Susan was unusually bright—with a rebel streak that made her demand being taught long division, after being told by her male teacher that the subject was too difficult for girls.

Upon becoming a teacher herself, Susan had briefly put aside plain Quaker gray in favor of stylish plum-colored silk and she had even taken up dancing. But at a ball she attended, she had an unfortunate experience she referred to only guardedly in her diary. It appears that her partner must have got drunk, for she wrote: "My fancy for attending dances is fully satisfied. I certainly shall not attend another unless I can have a total abstinence man to accompany me, and not one whose highest delight is to make a fool of himself."

From then on, she devoted her free time to a group called the Daughters of Temperance, the female adjunct of a reformist organization seeking to ban all use of alcoholic beverages. Miss Anthony's work as the principal of the female department of a private academy in the town of Canajoharie, not far from Seneca Falls, absorbed only a portion of her prodigious energy. The rest she poured into such fervent involvement in her new cause that soon she irritated New York's Sons of Temperance.

It was not fitting, they told her, for a female to speak at any meeting where men were present. That infuriated Miss Anthony. But why was she surprised? Mrs. Stanton put the question on their first meeting—and within a few years Miss Anthony had transferred her full allegiance to the cause of woman's rights.

She quit her school post to travel continuously, setting up meetings, circulating petitions, tirelessly attempting to enlist new supporters. Sarcastic articles in the newspapers, poking fun at the female "insurrection," did not make her task easier. Nevertheless, she could not stay discouraged because she kept on finding thoughtful women willing to join in the campaign.

Yet it was probably quite a narrow segment of the population that approved of woman suffrage in this early period. Many of the supporters had started, like Mrs. Mott and Miss Anthony, by enlisting in the anti-slavery or temperance movements, then turned to feminism after receiving insulting treatment from their male colleagues. Other wives or sisters usually accepted the prevailing male viewpoint that women should not venture beyond their "proper" sphere of home and family concerns.

With the outbreak of the Civil War in 1861, even Mrs. Stanton decided to postpone seeking more converts. She and Miss Anthony established a new group they called the Woman's Loyal League. Ostensibly, its purpose was to prod President Lincoln into proclaiming immediate freedom for all slaves, but Lizzie Stanton also had an ulterior motive. It was to prove that women were capable of playing the game of practical politics. Toward that end, Susan B. set up committees of women in every state of the Union, charged with gathering signatures on petitions urging emancipation. Huge scrolls containing thousands of names began piling up at the league's cubbyhole office in New York City.

Senator Charles Sumner of Massachusetts, leader of the Republican faction pressing for swift action by the President, spurred the women on. "Send me the petitions as fast as received," he wrote from Washington. "They give me opportunities for speech." In an unmatched example of organizing talent, Miss Anthony sent him scrolls containing almost 40,000 signatures—and Mrs. Stanton exulted.

Wouldn't the Republican party repay this terrific assistance by sponsoring woman suffrage? Soon after the war ended, when Senator Sumner and his associates began pushing through an amendment to the Constitution making it a sacred principle of national policy that former slaves could not be denied the right to vote, Mrs. Stanton demanded: Why not women, too?

"Be patient," the Senator put her off. "It's the Negroes' hour."

Crushed with disappointment, Mrs. Stanton wrote to Miss Anthony that now they would not see success in their own lifetime. Now they must painstakingly build support for a separate amendment giving women the vote. Or, even harder, they would have to win the passage of suffrage amendments to the constitutions of every state. For all her bold words in the past, Mrs. Stanton had never previously faced the harsh political truth that men were not going to give up their special privileges—unless they were somehow forced to.

If Lizzie Stanton had realized that fifty-six major battles lay ahead before suffrage would be won, perhaps even she would have surrendered during the years immediately following the Civil War. But she and Susan B. Anthony both were blessed with dauntless optimism. When an unexpected flash of marvelous news arrived from the West in 1869, these mature women behaved like a pair of giddy girls.

The Wyoming Territory had adopted the nation's first woman suffrage law! Mrs. Stanton was fifty-four years old, with snowy hair and a plump, grandmotherly figure, but she danced a jig. The staid Miss Anthony hugged everyone in sight. "It's the beginning!" she cried.

During the next several decades, as the United States expanded into a vast industrial nation stretching from the Atlantic to the Pacific, there were a few other similar celebrations. One by one, the new state constitutions of Colorado, Wyoming, Idaho, and Utah each allowed their women to vote, and no dire consequences to wholesome family life could be discovered, even though antisuffragists refused to admit this.

But in the rest of the country, the cause gradually floundered after male voters had turned down woman suffrage in Kansas and several other states. To convince a majority of the men in one state after another to vote yes at special elections on the issue was proving even harder than Mrs. Stanton had anticipated. Still, a less impatient wing of the woman suffrage movement, led by Lucy Stone of Massachusetts, insisted that the state-by-state procedure sooner or later would prevail.

Meanwhile, from about 1880 onward, during every session of Congress a California Senator named Sargent began intro-

A nineteenth-century cartoon captioned "Ye May Session of Ye Woman's Rights Convention—Ye Orator of Ye Day Denouncing Ye Lords of Creation." *Courtesy Library of Congress*

ducing a bill providing for a woman suffrage amendment to the Federal Constitution. Since Susan Anthony always led the delegation of women testifying in favor, it became generally known as "the Anthony amendment." Its text was simple:

> The right of citizens of the United States to vote shall not be denied or abridged by the United States or by any State on account of sex.

Year after year, the public hearings on the amendment were timed to coincide with the annual convention in Washington of the National Woman Suffrage Association. Yet there were plenty of opposing speakers, too, including many Senators from the conservative South who would stand and make statements like:

> For my part I want when I go to my home—when I turn from the arena where man contends with man for what we call the prizes of this paltry world—I want to go back, not to the embrace of some female ward politician, but to the earnest loving look and touch of some true woman. I want to go back to the jurisdiction of the wife, the mother; and instead of a lecture upon finance or the tariff, or upon the construction of the Constitution, I want those blessed loving details of domestic life and domestic love.

Faced with such sentiments, Miss Anthony and her associates made little headway. Every year, new hearings were held in Washington, but they failed to generate any new arguments. Now the leaders of the cause were old women, who seemed like quaint voices out of the past. Nearing her eighty-seventh birthday, Mrs. Stanton died in 1902. Miss Anthony, who had been more in the public eye, kept appearing at meetings for another few years. When she died in 1906, at the age of eighty-six, it became obvious that her single-hearted devotion to suffrage had won her an enormous amount of respectful admiration, despite her failure to achieve her goal. "The greatest woman produced by the New World," the San Francisco *Bulletin* called her.

There were some who mourned that her cause had died with her. Yet the opening years of the twentieth century saw many signs of a new spirit of reform around the United States. Gradually, quite a number of the restrictive laws or customs defining woman's "proper" sphere had been eased, making it possible for girls to be better educated and to enter professions from which they had previously been barred.

Now these pioneering women lawyers and professors and social workers were starting to ask each other: *Why* couldn't they vote? Also, the women's clubs becoming active in many states were convincing dozens of communities to let women cast ballots at least for the members of school boards or other local bodies. And suddenly, at this seeming low ebb in the national suffrage movement, startling news arrived from a most unexpected quarter.

It came from England, where the first reports about the Seneca Falls convention had inspired the start of a similar campaign. Particularly in the industrial city of Manchester, some earnest reformers—men, as well as women—had devoted much effort to promoting the cause. The main thing they accomplished, though, was to fire up the imagination of a fourteen-year-old girl who attended one of their meetings.

Now Mrs. Emmeline Pankhurst had two grown daughters of her own, Christabel and Sylvia. The three of them had been thrilled, in 1899, to meet their heroine Miss Susan Anthony, who had toured Britain speaking at suffrage gatherings when she was nearly eighty. The visit impelled Mrs. Pankhurst to think hard about how to stir up some real excitement.

Soon she and her daughters resigned from the established suffrage society, explaining that it had grown too stodgy over the years. They founded a new group, the Women's Social and Political Union, with the motto "Deeds Not Words!" After just a few years, Mrs. Pankhurst and her "wild women" began making headlines on both sides of the Atlantic.

Forcing the British government to cease ignoring the suffrage issue, women dressed as men and smuggled suffrage banners into political meetings, then unfurled them just as the Prime Minister began to speak. They paraded outside of Parliament. When such efforts failed to change official minds, the Pankhursts and their supporters began throwing stones—insisting that breaking some windows of government buildings was a valid form of political protest.

Of course, the women stone-throwers were arrested. Dozens of women, including all three Pankhursts, were flung into jail cells with common criminals. Incensed at not receiving the better treatment that political prisoners usually were granted, the women refused to eat. At that period, the only method of forcibly feeding a determined hunger-striker was extremely unpleasant. When the mighty British government, exalted around the world as a great civilizing influence, began forcibly feeding hundreds of women, even anti-suffragists were horrified.

But on both sides of the ocean, many people were just as distressed by the spectacle of women behaving in such an unladylike manner. Possibly, even Susan Anthony herself might have disapproved of Mrs. Pankhurst's militant tactics. Even so, there could be no disputing that the "Deeds Not Words!" in England had swiftly taken suffrage out of the category of just a quaint idea and turned it into a page-one issue.

All of this publicity stirred new sparks of life at the American National Woman Suffrage Association. In 1909, the irrepressible Mrs. Pankhurst came to the United States on a lecture tour. "I am what you call a hooligan," she cheerfully introduced herself to audiences in Boston, New York, Baltimore, and Chicago. The shouts of laughter this brought provided a novelty to suffrage supporters, for it had been a long time since they had had much to laugh about.

So even though old-line leaders of the cause in the United States took a dim view of Mrs. Pankhurst's methods, younger women murmured that a new century required new strategy. By 1912, when Mrs. Pankhurst returned for more lecturing, she found quite a different atmosphere.

Women decked out with sandwich-style picket signs marched up and down the main streets of the cities she visited, advertising her meetings. Banners informed her that the state of Washington had just voted in favor of woman suffrage, and so had California—the largest prize so far, after a suffrage campaign unmatched for its enthusiasm.

Then on Election Day of 1912, Arizona and Kansas and Oregon voted yes to suffrage. To celebrate this rising tide, several thousand marchers gathered for a joyous torchlight parade in New York City. During the next few months, though, younger members of the national suffrage organization held a series of worried private discussions.

Their careful study of political currents around the country had pointed toward a strange phenomenon. If the state-by-state approach were continued, it appeared likely that most of the women who lived west of the Mississippi River would be voting in another few years, while few if any of their sisters east of the Mississippi would enjoy the same privilege.

Wouldn't this be terribly unfair? It seemed urgent to resume pressure for amending the Federal Constitution—strong, unyielding pressure. Toward that goal, a quiet sort of coup was engineered whereby the most talented potential "general" in the suffrage ranks was drafted to direct an intense new drive for adoption of the Anthony amendment.

She was Carrie Chapman Catt, a former teacher from Iowa with a magnetic personality. An imposing woman in her middle fifties, Mrs. Catt had a great gift for jotting down exactly what had to be done in the notebook she always carried—then making sure each item on her list was assigned to some capable assistant. It was December of 1915 when Mrs. Catt assumed command, and during 1916 the American suffrage movement really started rolling toward victory.

As Mrs. Catt herself said in one of her rousing speeches that year: "There is one thing mightier than kings or armies, congresses or political parties—the power of an idea when its time has come to move."

Still, her own leadership certainly deserved much of the credit for suffrage's accomplishments preceding the presidential election of 1916. So, too, did the militant marches sponsored by a smaller and more radical group under the direction of Alice Paul, who had spent several years in England absorbing lessons from Mrs. Pankhurst. Above all, though, the enlistment of millions of wives and working women, poor and rich, changed what had been the project of just one segment of the middle class into a genuine mass movement.

For whatever reason, the platform committees at the national conventions of both the Republican and Democratic parties in the summer of 1916 came very close to endorsing the Anthony amendment outright, despite still bitter opposition from their conservative wings.

Then the Democratic President Wilson, running for re-election, became the first chief executive ever to address a suffrage gathering when he spoke on the same platform with Mrs. Catt that autumn. "I have not come to ask you to be patient," he said, "because you have been." Still, he, too, stopped short of giving the movement his full support because he dared not antagonize die-hard anti-suffragists in several Southern states upon whose votes his party depended.

Yet Mrs. Catt and her closest aides smiled confidently. Behind a closed door, they had just adopted a secret "plan of action," based on the fact that the year 1920 would mark the one hundredth anniversary of Susan Anthony's birth. By 1920, they had vowed, every woman in the United States would have the right to vote.

So in barber shops and at baseball games, wherever men congregated, they encountered groups of women wearing the yellow-ribbon sash that had become the badge of the suffragists. Wives and daughters of bankers and bootblacks wore their yellow ribbons in parades down the main streets of cities and towns from coast to coast. Most important, every member of Congress received a stream of polite but determined female callers.

This effort to secure Congressional support was the biggest lobbying campaign the country had ever seen. The women who took part in it made no threats but, by 1917, the list of states that had separately adopted suffrage had grown to the point where a substantial number of elected representatives could not help sensing an implied threat. If they chose to vote against the Anthony amendment when it came up for Congressional consideration, as it surely would very soon, clearly their own chances for being reelected would be sharply reduced.

Then, late in 1917, the most populous state in the nation—with the biggest Congressional delegation in Washington—gave the suffrage cause its greatest boost. Just two months after New York acted, in January of 1918 the House of Representatives put aside pressing business concerning the world war the country had recently entered to take a historic vote. Only once before, in 1915, had suffrage reached the voting stage in the House. Then the proposition that the Anthony amendment should be submitted to the states had won a majority vote but did not carry; on such questions, a full two-thirds affirmative tally was required.

But in 1918, exactly the required two-thirds did support suffrage. As the result became clear, a woman's voice up in the gallery rose in reverent song: "Praise God from whom all blessings flow." Many other voices joined in the hymn, producing a spontaneous chorus that those present would never forget.

By a remarkable coincidence, on the very same day, 3,000 miles away in London, Britain's House of Lords also voted in favor of woman suffrage. The House of Commons there had already given in, so the battle was won in Britain. But victory in the United States had not yet been assured. There was still the Senate to convince—and then the legislatures of at least thirty-six states.

Nevertheless, Mrs. Catt issued a jubilant statement: "The women of America will be voters in 1920, the one hundredth anniversary of the birth of Susan B. Anthony." Her disclosure of her secret timetable made headlines, and yet the Senate could not be swayed so easily.

Since the rules of the Senate gave ample leeway to those preferring delay, it was September of 1918 before the subject of suffrage even came up for debate. Then President Wilson himself drove down Pennsylvania Avenue to tell the lawmakers in person that he had changed his own mind and now supported suffrage fully as a vital step in the war effort. How could the United States claim it was fighting to make the world safe for democracy unless it treated its women fairly?

Even so, the Senate vote that September was two short of the required two-thirds majority. Swiftly Mrs. Catt issued some new orders. Four of the Senators who had voted against suffrage were coming up for reelection in November in states where women could vote. Defeat them, Mrs. Catt told her army of suffragists. Alice Paul, who now called her own group the Woman's Party, gave the same instructions. Two of the four did lose, while the other two won by only narrow margins.

On June 4, 1919, when the Senate voted again on suffrage, it finally passed—and the proposed Nineteenth Amendment could be sent to the legislatures of the several states for ratifying.

Mrs. Catt had a new notebook ready—a small black book with a few pages for every state. Immediately after the Senate acted, she telegraphed every governor asking the promptest possible action on ratification. Their replies were entered in her little black book.

Guided by her jottings, Mrs. Catt and teams of trusted aides then began a frantic round of travel. Although it had seemed likely that Wyoming would be the first to ratify, the honor went instead to Wisconsin, which acted within the same week of the Senate approval. Illinois and Michigan also approved the amendment almost as soon.

From then on, a tense series of appeals pressed other governors to convene their legislatures. By September of 1919, only thirteen had approved the amendment. By January of 1920, the number had risen to twenty-seven. On March 22, the state of Washington moved into line, becoming number thirty-five. Which state could be counted on to be the crucial thirty-sixth?

It proved to be Tennessee. After much hectic politicking, early in August of 1920 Tennessee ratified the suffrage amendment and formal notice of this action was transmitted to Washington. Then the Nineteenth Amendment was declared the law of the land, and women all over the country began registering to vote in the presidential election that November.

One of these new voters was an old lady past her ninetieth birthday. In upstate New York, Charlotte Woodward told interviewers about the summer day back in 1848 when she and other farm girls had driven into town to attend Mrs. Stanton's first meeting:

> I do clearly remember the wonderful beauty of the early morning when we dropped all our allotted tasks and climbed into the family wagon to drive over the rough roads to Seneca Falls. At first we traveled quite alone under the overhanging tree branches and wild vines, but before we had gone many miles we came on other wagonloads of women, bound in the same direction. As we reached different crossroads, we saw wagons coming from every part of the county, and long before we reached Seneca Falls we were a procession. . . .

12

From FDR to LBJ

It was March 4, 1933. At the depth of the Great Depression, when about half of the entire population of the United States belonged to families whose wage-earners could not find work, a man with a jaunty smile stood on the Capitol steps in Washington and promised to preserve, protect, and defend the nation's Constitution. Right after taking the oath that made him President, Franklin Delano Roosevelt leaned toward the vast crowd facing him and jutted forth his chin.

"First of all," he said, "let me assert my firm belief that the only thing we have to fear is fear itself."

These ringing words, carried by radio to every part of the land, raised a ripple of hope that kept growing stronger during one of the most remarkable periods in American history. Yet FDR's bold New Deal measures for counteracting the worst economic crisis ever to confront the country also ushered in an era of great constitutional turmoil.

Fittingly, even the date on which Roosevelt took up residence in the White House would be notable to the compilers of constitutional lore. While every President since George Washington had assumed office on March 4, FDR would be the last to be inaugurated on that date. At least in this case, however, the break with tradition had not been initiated by FDR himself.

The preceding year, in March of 1932, Congress itself had proposed the Twentieth Amendment to the Constitution, one of the least controversial ever to be put forward. Back in the days when travel had been much more difficult and time-consuming, it had made sense to allow four months between Election Day and the assumption of office by the new President and the new Congress. But holding to the old practice had produced a most unpopular political animal— the "lame duck."

This was the term applied to lawmakers and even chief executives who remained in office after everybody knew they would be relegated to has-beens as soon as the next spring rolled around. Because lame ducks were far from effective in running the government, practically everybody agreed on the need for a change, and the first steps were taken during the conservative administration of the Republican President Herbert Hoover. Ratifications by state legislatures went so fast that the Democratic FDR almost, but not quite, became eligible for inauguration on January 20 in 1933.

As it worked out, though, when he overwhelmingly won a second term in 1936, his second inauguration—on January 20, 1937—would mark the first use of the new date. By then, Roosevelt had already guaranteed that, by his own actions, he would go down in constitutional texts for much more significant reasons. Right from the outset of his first term, he daringly steered a course that was bound to bring a series of collisions with "standpatters" on the Supreme Court.

Starting with a breathtaking rush of emergency programs during the famous Hundred Days of a special session of Congress, FDR increased the scope of the federal government far beyond any previous administration. Aided by a "Brains Trust" of professors, he proposed dozens of economic and welfare plans aimed at ending the terrible Depression. Among all these departures from the laissez faire policies of the past, none made more headlines than the National Industrial Recovery Act.

Under this law, an agency called the National Recovery Administration—immediately tagged the NRA—encouraged every sort of business to adopt codes forbidding a long list of unfair practices and guaranteeing employees fair working conditions. By raising standards throughout American industry, the New Deal theorists insisted, consumers as well as workers and their bosses all would benefit.

President Roosevelt himself described the law establishing the NRA as "the most important and far-reaching legislation ever enacted by the American Congress." Amid much public enthusiasm, companies complying with the new codes displayed the NRA symbol of a Blue Eagle emblazoned with the motto: "We Do Our Part." Still, as the complications and complexities of regulating the entire range of commerce became increasingly apparent, criticism of the NRA mounted.

The basic question went back to the Constitution. Could its clause granting Congress the power to regulate interstate commerce authorize such expansion of federal action as the diverse codes of the NRA? Yet the answer, once more, depended on another question. Would the Supreme Court take a broad or a narrow view in interpreting the NRA's constitutionality?

There had, of course, been seesaw swings between the two extremes throughout the nation's history. But on the Supreme Court bench at the beginning of Roosevelt's tenure in the White House, four of the justices were known to be diehard conservatives. Although three others had a somewhat liberal bent, the remaining two struck most observers as more likely to support their conservative brethren than to side with the liberals.

So the prospects for high court approval of any New Deal measure were not too strong. Since the court does not issue pronouncements until a case involving a constitutional question is begun by some citizen or group, and then goes through various preliminaries, it took almost two years until the expected conflict actually got underway. In January of 1935, the first New Deal statute to come up for judicial review was struck down as unconstitutional.

During the following sixteen months, another ten major cases or groups of cases also reached the court—and eight of the ten decisions outlawed important New Deal programs. Besides the Agricultural Adjustment Act, setting up innovative ways of helping the nation's farmers, laws involving such varied matters as coal mining and pensions for railroad workers were all invalidated. Yet the decision on the fate of the NRA probably had the greatest emotional impact.

"The Case of the Sick Chicken," some newspapers tagged the NRA test that was argued before the Supreme Court during the spring of 1935. More formally, *Schechter v. U.S.* had been brought by a firm of New York poultry dealers claiming that the NRA code regulating their trade represented an unwarranted interference in local commerce. Despite a certain amount of comic testimony regarding diseased birds, the case produced a verdict Chief Justice Charles Evans Hughes read aloud very solemnly.

"Extraordinary conditions do not create or enlarge constitutional power," Hughes asserted in an opinion endorsed unanimously by all nine justices. The lack of any dissent gave this ruling added weight because most of the previous anti-New Deal decisions had come in split votes, sometimes as close as five to four.

Further adding to the significance of the NRA opinion, Justice Hughes took the narrowest possible view of the specific constitutional question under consideration. Brushing aside testimony that most of the chickens sold in New York were shipped in from other states, he concentrated instead on the point that the Schechters themselves sold only to New York customers.

"So far as the poultry here in question is concerned," Hughes held, "the flow in interstate commerce had ceased. The poultry had come to a permanent rest within the State." Therefore, Congress could not legally regulate the way the Schechters did business—and the whole NRA was invalid.

Roosevelt did not take the defeat lightly. Lecturing reporters attending one of his press conferences, he accused the Supreme Court of attempting to transport the country back to "the horse-and-buggy days." Then as the high court kept overturning other laws, the wily FDR commenced thinking about how he might outwit "the nine old men"—his own scornful phrase, referring to the fact that six of the nine justices were already past the age of seventy. Being an avid student of history, he was well aware that members of the federal judiciary held lifetime appointments in keeping with Article III of the Constitution, and that some had continued serving well into their eighties.

But Roosevelt refused to accept the prospect that practically every New Deal experiment might be outlawed. He saw the Supreme Court as the last-ditch defender of unfettered free enterprise, benefiting mainly big corporations and their wealthy owners. Despite his own privileged upbringing, he had based his whole program on improving the lot of "the common man."

No matter if these words may sound condescending half a century later, in the 1930s FDR's warm, sure voice and his willingness to try new ways of restoring prosperity exerted a magical appeal. So the presidential election of 1936 won him a second term by the largest margin any candidate had ever received. Exhilarated by this unprecedented victory, Roosevelt proceeded soon after his second inauguration to propose an amazing plan for thwarting his enemies on the Supreme Court.

Early in 1937, he blandly sent Congress a bill for "reorganizing" the court to improve its efficiency. The core of his plan empowered the President to take a decisive step whenever any justice failed to resign within six months after reaching his seventieth birthday. In that eventuality, the President could appoint one additional justice—and the only limit on this new appointment power was that no more than fifteen justices could occupy the bench simultaneously, instead of the long-prevailing maximum of nine.

The outcry provoked by this idea stunned FDR. For once, his usually uncanny political sense had led him into a complete miscalculation. While opposition from the Republican minority that was already irate over many New Deal measures surely could have been expected, neither the President nor any of his most loyal supporters had anticipated the furor his plan to "pack" the Supreme Court aroused among Democrats, too.

Suddenly, it seemed that people from every walk of life felt as if a sacred feature of the American government were being threatened. To constitutional experts, the fuss over

At the height of the controversy over President Franklin D. Roosevelt's plan to "pack" the Supreme Court, a cartoonist pictured him as having tossed the Constitution into a waste basket. *Courtesy Franklin D. Roosevelt Library*

preserving the membership of the highest court at no more than nine justices appeared rather misguided because that number was not even mentioned in the Constitution. Setting the size of the Supreme Court had been left to Congress and, over the years, the original contingent of six justices had been changed several times before eventually being stabilized at nine.

Still, the experts perceived the widespread outrage as a sign that the public had come to regard the nation's highest court with deep respect. Despite frequent dissension over its rulings, the notion of tampering with its exalted status above ordinary political frays obviously frightened thoughtful citizens, no matter what their own party affiliation might be. They worried that the court would no longer be able to exercise independent judgment if any President held such power to pick new justices who shared his own outlook.

So even though some Roosevelt supporters in Congress went through the motions of trying to pass the court-packing scheme, it never came up for an actual vote. The Senate committee charged with judiciary affairs refused to recommend it, and in July of 1937, the Senate as a whole voted seventy to twenty in favor of letting the committee simply bury the whole idea.

This defeat marked a notable turning point for President Roosevelt himself. While his huge popularity among rank-and-file Democrats soon was restored, he faced increasing obstruction from conservative members of his own party in Congress. Many Republicans regarded him with extreme distrust or outright hatred. Refusing even to speak his name, they referred to him furiously as "that man in the White House."

Nevertheless, Roosevelt could not really regret raising the issue, for at the height of the Supreme Court controversy, quite a startling change occurred in the thinking of two of the justices. Several new cases arose involving major New Deal measures, and these two men found it possible to join with their three liberal-minded colleagues in upholding the New Deal viewpoint.

But what had caused this strange reversal? Most observers traced it to a feature of American democracy that had been seen more than once down through the years—the tendency of wise judges to reconsider their own social philosophy if their opinions appeared to place them too far off the governmental path of a chief executive who had just been re-elected. At any rate, in the next few years the death or retirement of several justices gave President Roosevelt ample opportunities to appoint replacements he could count on to back up his programs.

So FDR "had lost a battle and won a war," as one authority put it. Indeed, from the spring of 1937 onward there was such a revolutionary change in the tenor of Supreme Court decisions that law students are taught to consider the year one of the most important milestones in constitutional history.

Ever since the Civil War, the Supreme Court had mostly used its power of judicial review to foster a very strict interpretation of some of the language of the Constitution, especially phrases concerning interstate commerce and the general welfare. Then, almost overnight, during Franklin Roosevelt's second term the court set aside seventy years of precedents and began stretching those words as if they had almost unlimited elasticity.

The effect of all this broadening was to establish a new era of federal predominance—the age of "big government" in Washington. But our focus here is on the Constitution itself, so another by-product of FDR's presidency must now be considered. As early as the spring of 1937, a great new guessing game had begun engrossing the nation.

"Mr. President," a reporter had asked then, "would you care to comment on the governor of Pennsylvania's suggestion that you run for a third term?"

Flashing his beaming smile, FDR remarked, "The weather is very hot today."

From then on, similar exchanges fascinated—and infuriated—the American people. Ever since George Washington had declined to run for a third term, no man had served more than eight years as the nation's chief executive. Even if the Constitution had nothing to say on the subject, such a long-standing tradition exerted a powerful influence. Yet FDR's immensely magnetic personality not only attracted millions of voters with a force far beyond any other public figure, but also repelled some Americans just as strongly.

Possibly, Roosevelt himself would rather have retired to his Hudson River estate in 1940. That was what he told a few friends, while keeping the nation guessing. But the course of events in Europe, where the Second World War had recently erupted, threatened the United States to such an extent that the Democratic National Convention "drafted" FDR to run again, and he proved unbeatable.

Although Roosevelt's third-term victory came by a much narrower margin than his two previous triumphs, his brilliant war leadership after the United States did become involved in the fighting impressed even his political enemies. In 1944, another presidential election year, as the worldwide conflict approached a critical stage there was less controversy when FDR sought and won a fourth term.

Worn by the pressures of his high office during twelve years of unparalleled domestic and foreign crisis, Roosevelt collapsed only a few months after his fourth inauguration. The news of his sudden death, on April 12, 1945, brought a great wave of grief in every part of the globe, for he had been loved as few political figures have ever been loved.

Yet the negative emotions he had also inspired did not die

President Franklin D. Roosevelt in a relaxed moment during his third term in the White House. *Courtesy Franklin D. Roosevelt Library*

with him. Two years later, in 1947 a Republican-controlled
Congress proposed a new amendment to the Constitution
that supposedly had a patriotic motive. There could not be
the slightest doubt, however, that its underlying purpose
was to achieve a long-unsatisfied revenge against a leader
who had been invincible in his own lifetime. For the
Twenty-second Amendment's crucial words were:

> No person shall be elected to the office of the President more
> than twice. . . .

It took four years until a sufficient number of states
ratified the amendment to make it part of the supreme law of
the land in 1951. Ironically, this anti-Roosevelt addition to
the Constitution turned into a sort of political boomerang,
thwarting the very party that had sponsored it. Many people
thought the tremendously popular Republican President
Dwight Eisenhower might well have won a third term in
1960, if no two-term limit had been adopted. Moreover, the
same amendment would guarantee the retirement of another
seemingly unbeatable Republican when Ronald Reagan confronted the third-term prohibition during the 1980s.

Much before then, however, two less controversial additions to the Constitution had been ratified with hardly any
dissension, and another major change affecting the executive
branch of the federal government had taken effect, too.

In 1961, a long-standing restriction on democratic procedure was erased when the Twenty-third Amendment allowed residents of the District of Columbia to vote in
presidential elections and for local officials. Previously this
area between Maryland and Virginia, which had become the
site of the nation's capital, had been ruled by Congress,
without any participation on the part of its own populace.

Three years later, in 1964, the Twenty-fourth Amendment

finally ended a different kind of restraint on the right to vote. Back in the 1800s, many states had charged a so-called poll tax, aimed at preventing the poor from casting ballots. Only a few states still preserved some vestige of this once-prevalent device, used most often in the South as a weapon against black voters, when the ban became effective during the presidency of Lyndon Baines Johnson.

A far more significant constitutional change also came while LBJ was in the White House. The Twenty-fifth Amendment, one of the most complicated ever adopted, aimed to solve a variety of problems involving presidential disability and succession. Unhappily, the stimulus for clarifying what should be done if a chief executive could no longer serve had arisen out of the assassination of President John F. Kennedy in 1963.

As it so tragically happened, Kennedy had died immediately and Vice President Johnson had been sworn in as his successor less than two hours later. But if the assassin's bullet had seriously and yet not fatally wounded the nation's leader, how would the country have been governed? Just such a situation had already occurred nearly a century earlier, when President James Garfield had remained incapacitated for more than two months before dying of complications from a shot fired by a disappointed office seeker. In that simpler era, the United States had lacked any hand at the helm until Vice President Chester Arthur finally took over after Garfield's death.

Not merely the terrible specter of violence, though, inspired the Twenty-fifth Amendment. Similar crises could arise if the occupant of the White House were to become seriously disabled by accident or some disease. Indeed, the acute illness of President Wilson back in 1919 had made constitutional experts realize how inadequate the original docu-

ment was as a guide for coping with such emergencies. All it
had to say on the subject was:

> In case of the removal of the President from office, or of his
> death, resignation, or inability to discharge the powers and
> duties of the said office, the same shall devolve on the Vice
> President. . . .

The remainder of the clause gave Congress the power,
should both the President and Vice President be unavaila-
ble, of "declaring what officer shall then act as President"
until the next regular election. Yet no machinery existed
whereby an ailing chief executive could be supplanted—
temporarily or permamently—if he himself did not admit his
"inability" to discharge his duties.

In the absence of any such constitutional provision, a
nearly incredible makeshift arrangement had prevailed in
Washington during the last year and a half of President
Wilson's second term. Owing to the greater privacy enjoyed
by inhabitants of the White House then, the full story was
not told until after the lapse of several decades. At the time,
official announcements repeatedly assured the public that
the President was attending to business upstairs while re-
covering from "nervous exhaustion" caused by overwork.

Yet he had really suffered a series of strokes, leaving him
partly paralyzed and very weak. Undoubtedly, it was his wife
who refused to let the truth be known because she feared
that the impact of alarming publicity would be more than
her intensely conscientious husband could endure. Perhaps
she even refused to believe the truth herself.

If she acted out of love, the behavior of the President's
closest aides and of his personal physician must be blamed
more on a misguided sense of loyalty. Taking their cue from
Mrs. Wilson, they engaged in what amounted to a conspir-

acy, with the goal of keeping Wilson at least nominally at the head of the government.

Only years afterward would it come out that at a Cabinet meeting soon after the President was stricken, the Secretary of State pointedly read aloud the phrase in the Constitution regarding presidential disability. Then Wilson's closest assistant coldly asked who could certify to the President's disability. As for himself, he said, he would take no part in any effort to "oust" him.

"And I am sure," he added, "that Dr. Grayson will never certify to his disability." Turning toward the physician, he demanded, "Will you, Grayson?" Grayson shook his head.

The result was that Mrs. Wilson became, in effect, the Acting President. She stood guard over her husband's bedroom, deciding what messages should be brought in to him. As his strength revived slightly, she decided who should or should not be allowed to pay him a brief visit. Eventually, the First Lady herself began telling some callers what "the President wanted" done on some particular matter.

Despite all the reassurances about Wilson's continued improvement, something of the real state of affairs did penetrate beyond the White House. At a committee meeting, Senator Albert Fall of New Mexico lost his temper one day. "We have petticoat government!" he shouted. "Mrs. Wilson is President!"

In the years that followed, even though no such dramatic instance of presidential disability occurred, there was increasing concern over presidential health as the spotlight of national attention shone more and more on the White House. After Franklin Roosevelt's death, some people wondered whether he had actually been fit to embark on the rigors of a fourth term.

But the health issue assumed much greater weight during

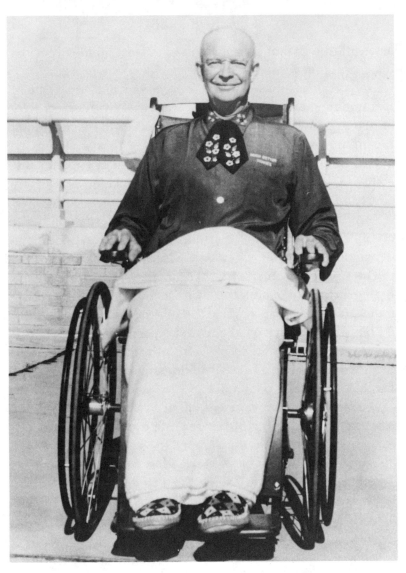

President Dwight D. Eisenhower posing for photographers during one of the illnesses that marked his presidency. Embroidered on his shirt are the words, "Much better, thanks." *Courtesy Dwight D. Eisenhower Library*

the presidency of Dwight Eisenhower, when he suffered three different ailments over the course of his eight years in office—a heart attack in 1955, then an intestinal obstruction requiring major surgery the following year, and a slight stroke a year later in 1957. Fortunately, he recovered quite rapidly from each of these conditions.

During Eisenhower's three brief periods of incapacity, Vice President Richard Nixon was careful not to seem bent on displacing him. Yet the spectacle of a hospitalized chief executive was deeply impressed on the public consciousness by the new medium of television. Discussion about amending the Constitution to set precise procedures for dealing with any future cases of presidential disability inevitably followed.

Then came the shocking murder of President Kennedy on November 22, 1963. Only forty-six years old at the time of his death, he had been the youngest man ever elected to serve in the White House. As the result of the national trauma his assassination caused, a patchwork of laws and informal letters of understanding finally was superceded in 1967 by the ratification of the Twenty-fifth Amendment. Its various clauses provided new ways to meet different eventualities, such as:

> Whenever there is a vacancy in the office of the Vice President, the President shall nominate a Vice President who shall take office upon confirmation by a majority vote of both houses of Congress.

Thanks to this provision, President Richard Nixon was able in 1973 to select Congressman Gerald Ford of Michigan as his Vice President after his elected running mate, Spiro Agnew, had resigned under the cloud of a scandal involving acceptance of bribes. When Ford himself succeeded to the Presidency after Nixon's resignation—at the height of the even more shocking Watergate scandal threatening him with impeachment—Ford chose Governor Nelson Rockefeller of New York as *his* Vice President.

Beyond establishing an indisputable procedure for filling vacancies in the offices of President and Vice President, the Twenty-fifth also prescribed:

> Whenever the President transmits to the President pro tempore of the Senate and the Speaker of the House of Representatives his written declaration that he is unable to discharge the powers and duties of his office, and until he transmits to them a written declaration to the contrary, such powers and duties shall be discharged by the Vice President.

This was the clause that would be invoked briefly, in 1985, when President Ronald Reagan faced surgery to remove a cancer. But in still more of a departure from the uncertainties of the past, the amendment sought to avoid any future case similar to that of Woodrow Wilson by adding:

> Whenever the Vice President and a majority of either the principal officers of the executive departments or of such other body as Congress may by law provide, transmit to the President pro tempore of the Senate and the Speaker of the House of Representatives their written declaration that the President is unable to discharge the powers and duties of his office, the Vice President shall immediately assume the powers and duties of the office as Acting President.

Then, should the President later claim no inability existed, he would resume his duties—unless the Vice President and a majority of the Cabinet or some other body set up by Congress submitted a written protest, holding the President still unable to perform his functions. "Thereupon," the Twenty-fifth provided, "Congress shall decide the issue."

In the same period when all the complexities of presidential disability were occupying the Congressional framers of this important amendment to the Constitution, other far-ranging decisions were being arrived at by the Supreme Court itself. From the Eisenhower years through LBJ's tenure as chief executive, a whole new chapter was being written under the leadership of Chief Justice Earl Warren. It is time now to consider the sweeping changes that "The Warren Court" wrought.

13

The Warren Court

IN 1953, PRESIDENT EISENHOWER chose a rather unusual way of removing a potential rival from the political arena. He appointed this popular fellow-Republican to a post traditionally insulated from partisan strife—as Chief Justice of the United States. It was an appointment that surprised many people.

Earl Warren seemed, in 1953, to be just a big, friendly, white-haired man who liked politics. As governor of California, he had managed to please voters with liberal leanings while at the same time giving a safely conservative impression, so commentators expected him to run for President himself sooner or later. But most of them thought he lacked the solid legal training that would qualify him to head the country's highest court.

While he had often displayed an instinctive sense of fairness, it was his gift for making friends that had brought Warren his first public job—as an assistant to the district attorney of Alameda County, right across the bay from San Francisco. Then he spent twenty years in the post of district attorney there, which led to his election as California's attorney general. In 1942, he became governor of what was then the country's second most populous state.

Two successful terms in this office had turned Warren into a national figure. Even when he ran for Vice President in 1948 on the losing ticket headed by New York's Governor Thomas E. Dewey, his own popularity did not suffer. To most voters, though, he remained just an agreeable sort of man with moderate Republican views who was also the father of six exceptionally attractive blond and blue-eyed young Americans.

As it happened, however, Warren became a memorable—and also a very controversial—Chief Justice. During his sixteen years on the bench, he exerted more influence over the nation's course than many occupants of the White House ever have. With good reason, one writer entitled a book about him *The Judge Who Changed America*.

He began changing it less than a year after he assumed his new position. In the spring of 1954, a crucial case with the mild-sounding label of *Brown v. the Board of Education* forced the Supreme Court to confront a question involving intense emotions: Did the Constitution really allow public school systems to practice racial segregation?

Back in 1896, the justices then serving had set forth three words—"separate but equal"—as the test by which any claim of discriminatory treatment should be examined. This decision in the landmark case of *Plessy v. Ferguson* had done much more than merely deny a black man the right to ride in a railroad car reserved for white travelers. It had legalized separate facilities of all sorts if supposedly equal facilities were provided for blacks.

Earl Warren, Chief Justice of the United States from 1953 to 1969. *Courtesy Ankers Photographers, Inc.*

Since 1896, the feeling that *Plessy v. Ferguson* itself was a blot on American democracy had been gradually growing stronger. Despite implacable opposition by defenders of racial segregation—practiced openly in the South, but more subtle forms of racial prejudice infected the North, too—a small civil rights movement developed over the decades. Then simmering discontent about the subjugation of blacks boiled up as a by-product of World War II.

In that 1940s conflict, hundreds of thousands of black men donned uniforms to die for their country, if necessary. The distance between the nation's high ideals and its actual practice became painfully clear when black soldiers returned home to find the same old barriers preventing them from sharing the blessings of peace. Jobs, housing, even lunch counters at department stores, all were restricted; yet the educational disadvantages facing black children struck civil rights advocates as their most pressing problem.

In twenty-one states then, separate school systems were maintained for black children and white children. Despite the lip service to "separate but equal" facilities required by *Plessy v. Ferguson,* it was clear that black schools were inferior. They received smaller appropriations of money for buildings, books, and teachers' salaries than the white schools did. The teachers were not as well-prepared as those in the white schools.

Still, it was no easy matter to reverse a long-standing decision by the Supreme Court, especially on an issue provoking such an intensity of emotion. Two men of vastly different backgrounds would play leading roles in the drama—Earl Warren, the son of poor Norwegian immigrants, and Thurgood Marshall, the great-grandson of a slave.

But Oliver Brown, a black citizen of Topeka, Kansas, played an essential, if lesser part because he thought his eleven-year-old daughter Linda was not getting as good an education as the white children of their city. So he started a lawsuit, seeking to have Linda admitted to a white school. About the same time, similar cases were begun in four other school districts for the same purpose. By an alphabetical accident, because Brown's name led the list of plaintiffs when the group of five cases reached the Supreme Court, he and Linda became famous.

For *Brown v. the Board of Education* made history. It has affected every child, black or white, attending schools anywhere in the United States, and every parent, too. Also, it opened the way for more lawsuits by blacks seeking equal rights in housing, hotels, restaurants, and many other areas—rights that are taken for granted today, but which were not respected only a few decades ago.

Yet *Brown v. the Board of Education* did not just happen because the times were right. A good-humored but determined black lawyer—"Mr. Civil Rights," some newspapers would call him—was largely responsible for planning the strategy by which *Plessy v. Ferguson* might be overturned. He had dreamed of doing so ever since his boyhood in Baltimore when his father, who took charge of the restaurant at a country club for well-off whites, had given him the idea that he ought to study law.

"He never told me to become a lawyer, but he turned me into one," Thurgood Marshall would recall. "He did it by teaching me to argue, by challenging my logic on every point, by making me prove every statement I made."

His own state of Maryland required all black children to go to segregated schools, but the young Marshall was prodded into rising above his limited opportunities for learning by his mother, a teacher in the grade school he attended. After graduating from the all-black Lincoln University in Pennsylvania, he still was denied admission to the University of Maryland Law School because of the color of his skin. Instead, he earned his law degree at Howard University in Washington, D.C., one of the finest blacks-only institutions for higher learning then in existence.

As the top student in his class, Marshall attracted the attention of several professors closely connected with the group usually referred to as the NAACP—the National Association for the Advancement of Colored People. This was during the early 1930s, when President Franklin Roosevelt's New Deal had inspired glowing hopes among the reform-minded, and the NAACP was about to embark on a new drive toward reducing unfair treatment of black Americans. Soon after graduating, in 1935 Marshall went to work for the pioneering civil rights organization.

Three years later, Marshall became the head of the NAACP's legal staff. In effect, he spent the next sixteen years preparing—as he pressed one lesser case after another—for the day in 1954 when he stood up at the lawyer's table facing the nine justices of the Supreme Court and proceeded to tell them why they should outlaw racial segregation in the nation's schools.

The intent of the framers of the Fourteenth Amendment, Marshall insisted, had been "to prohibit all state action based on race or color." Boldly, he called upon the court to overrule the "separate but equal" opinion in *Plessy v. Ferguson* more than fifty years earlier.

One justice asked Marshall if he would still say that segregation in the schools was unconstitutional, should the states with separate educational systems agree to spend more money on improving schools for blacks.

Yes, Marshall replied firmly. He held that the Fourteenth Amendment guaranteed former slaves the full rights of citizenship, and that segregation actually was "a last vestige of slavery."

But lawyers representing some of the school systems involved contended it was not within the court's power to set aside long-standing practice that suited local conditions. A lawyer from Topeka told the justices that his city had already embarked on a voluntary plan for desegregating its schools. Another attorney representing the state of Kansas protested that federal interference in the state's schools was "neither necessary nor justified."

Yet a principle of great importance had been raised by the school desegregation case. When both sides had concluded their legal arguments, many people wondered during the several weeks that the justices were deliberating behind closed doors whether the court might decide, after all, to dodge the basic issue—or confront it squarely. There had rarely been a case before the highest court that aroused so much suspense concerning its verdict.

On May 17, 1954—a date that has gone down as one of the most significant in the annals of the Supreme Court— Chief Justice Warren read aloud the unanimous decision he and his colleagues had reached.

"We conclude," he said slowly and deliberately, "that in the field of public education, the doctrine of 'separate but equal' has no place." Then he went on:

> Separate educational facilities are inherently unequal. There-fore, we hold that the plaintiffs and others similarly situated . . . are, by reason of the segregation complained of, deprived of the equal protection of the laws guaranteed by the Fourteenth Amendment.

Chief Justice Warren's calm pronouncement opening a new era in race relations also marked the start of a new stage in his own life. Until then, people of every political persuasion had regarded him as an amiable candidate who was not particularly thoughtful—an attitude he encouraged by his good-natured jokes about having been only a "C" student back in his law school days at the University of California.

But when reporters scurried around trying to discover what lay behind the momentous reversal he had announced, they found evidence that Warren himself was a very skillful leader.

He had apparently spent several weeks conferring in private with his fellow justices, striving to smooth over any points of dissension so that they could present a unanimous verdict. Because the issue under consideration contained the seeds of such passionate dispute, he believed it was especially important to have the court united. Relying on bright young aides to find the appropriate legal language, the Chief Justice himself concentrated on using the same common-sense approach he had always found effective in the past.

But *Brown v. the Board of Education* began a remarkable process by which Earl Warren, at the age of sixty-three, was transformed simultaneously into a great hero and a terrible villain. Somehow, he managed to keep on following his own conscience despite the cheers and booing his every public appearance brought. Still, the full flowering of all this positive and negative celebrity did not occur immediately, just as it took time for the full impact of the anti-segregation decision to become apparent.

Because the Supreme Court recognized the complexity of revising educational injustice, in its historical ruling it called for further hearings about ways of carrying out the new policy it had mandated. A year later, in 1955, it established the guideline that desegregation of the schools should move forward "with all deliberate speed."

Yet despite the Supreme Court's exalted status as the supreme interpreter of what the Constitution means, it had no physical power to enforce its decisions. Carrying out its judgments rested on their acceptance by ordinary citizens and by public-officeholders who had sworn to uphold the

Constitution—a commitment including, most experts agreed, obedience to the verdicts of the nation's highest court.

On the issue of school segregation, the Supreme Court had spoken and its words were now the law of the land. Nevertheless, the decision stirred bitter opposition, particularly in the South. Bumper stickers began appearing on cars there bearing an ominous message: Impeach Earl Warren.

In plain fact, the decision on *Brown v. the Board of Education* did not mean that a single segregated school desegregated, that any blacks were admitted to previously all-white schools, or that any sort of integration automatically took place. The pace of desegregation was left up to individual states and to local school districts.

As a result, many school districts simply ignored the court decision, awaiting any further lawsuit that might force them into action. Others took only minimal action, giving token evidence of not disobeying the new policy. In Virginia, a campaign of massive resistance to the Supreme Court's order received official sanction when the state legislature passed a law forbidding any school board to integrate.

So a major constitutional crisis confronted the nation. During the next few years, it took armed intervention and the power of the Presidency to enforce the court's decision in several places.

On September 4, 1957—the first day of a new school year—nine black students attempted to enter Central High School in Little Rock, Arkansas, under a court order. They found themselves barred by units of the Arkansas National Guard, standing shoulder to shoulder around the building. After three weeks of legal maneuvering, the soldiers were removed and local police escorted the black students into the school while an angry mob shouted threats at them.

Soon, though, they were taken home again because the police were having trouble controlling the mob.

As a result, President Eisenhower sent troops of the 101st Airborne Division to Little Rock to maintain order and guarantee that the black children could attend school. With troops standing guard throughout the year to protect the black students, it was an atmosphere scarcely conducive to education. A federal district court described the situation that year at Central High as one of "chaos, bedlam, and turmoil," with repeated incidents of violence directed at the blacks.

Then the local school board asked permission to let the situation cool by postponing desegregation. But the Supreme Court ruled that the constitutional rights of the black children "are not to be sacrificed or yielded to the violence and disorder," which it blamed on actions of the state's governor and legislature.

In direct response to the defiant claim by lawyers representing Arkansas that it was not bound to obey the court, the court then added a stern warning: "No state legislator or executive or judicial officer can war against the Constitution without violating his undertaking to support it." The court went on to quote a famous statement by Chief Justice John Marshall:

> If the legislatures of the several states may, at will, annul the judgements of the courts of the United States, and destroy the rights acquired under those judgements, the Constitution itself becomes a mockery.

Despite these stern words, however, in Little Rock it obviously was presidential power—demonstrated by the use of armed force—that eventually brought compliance with the court's decision. Under the Constitution, the President is obligated to "take care that the laws be faithfully executed," and thus, by extension, to see that Supreme Court decisions are obeyed.

But no one can force the President to do so. Indeed, at two previous periods in American history a chief executive had refused to uphold a Supreme Court decision. Back in 1832, the court had issued an unpopular ruling involving Cherokee Indians in Georgia, and President Andrew Jackson was reported to have said: "Well, John Marshall has made his decision. Now let him enforce it." On another case concerning the Bank of the United States, Jackson had contended:

> The opinion of the judges has no more authority over Congress than the opinion of Congress has over judges, and on that point the President is independent of both. The authority of the Supreme Court must not, therefore, be permitted to control the Congress or the Executive when acting in their legislative capacities, but to have only such influence as the force of their reason deserves.

At a time of crisis, Abraham Lincoln had taken a similar position. Ignoring a Supreme Court order calling for the release of suspected traitors who had been arrested, Lincoln had explained: "I felt that measures, otherwise unconstitutional, might become lawful by becoming indispensable to the preservation of the Constitution through the preservation of the nation."

In Little Rock in 1957, President Eisenhower at first was reluctant to use force, but he did. Five years later his successor, President John F. Kennedy, also resorted to force in an integration case, this time in Mississippi.

When a federal court ordered the admission of James H. Meredith, a black Air Force veteran, to the University of

Mississippi, the governor of that state issued an official proc-
lamation attacking what he called "illegal use" of judicial de-
cree and refused to admit Meredith. President Kennedy
called in the National Guard and federal marshals, who had
to use tear gas to disperse protestors, before Meredith could
begin his studies.

A third major confrontation took place the following year,
in 1963, at the University of Alabama, when Governor
George Wallace himself stood in the doorway to bar the admission of two black students. But after this show of de-
fiance, the two students—protected by federal marshals—
peacefully enrolled there.

Those armed confrontations were only a few of the tense
episodes that marked the Warren Court years. It was a tu-
multuous period in which the Supreme Court became a sort
of super-legislature, decreeing major readjustments throughout the United States. All over the country, lower federal
courts followed the new policy set in Washington by drawing
new boundaries for local school districts, calculating percent-
ages of black and white children, even mapping bus routes
to achieve the racial balance the Supreme Court had ordered.

Important as the desegregation case was, however, it
turned out to be only one of the many controversial decisions during Chief Justice Warren's years on the bench. Under his leadership, the Supreme Court took a more active
role than ever before. Unlike previous courts that had
merely prohibited practices they deemed violations of the
Constitution, the Warren Court repeatedly commanded political bodies to correct practices that it had ruled unconstitutional.

In a series of decisions that are still hotly debated today,
the Warren Court expanded the rights of those accused of

crimes and ordered the redrawing of election districts so that all voters would have equal representation. Perhaps most controversial of all, it ruled that abortion clinics were legal—opening the way for a subsequent verdict broadening women's rights to end unwanted pregnancies after Warren himself retired. So the Warren Court significantly altered American life in many respects.

Among the most important criminal cases it considered was one involving a Cleveland woman named Dollree Mapp. In May 1957, two police officers had searched her house looking for a bombing suspect. They did not find him, but they did find some pornographic pictures, so she was arrested and convicted of possessing obscene materials. When she appealed to the Supreme Court, though, it reversed her conviction by a five-to-four vote, because it said the search of her home—conducted without a warrant issued by a judge—had been illegal. "All evidence obtained by searches and seizures in violation of the Constitution is, by that same authority, inadmissable in a state court," the Supreme Court ruled.

Another criminal case concerned Clarence Gideon, who had been convicted of breaking into a poolroom in Panama City, Florida. At his trial, he had asked for a lawyer but his request was denied. From jail, he sent a handwritten appeal to the Supreme Court. It appointed an eminent attorney—Abe Fortas, later a Supreme Court justice himself—to represent Gideon. After hearing his arguments, the court agreed in 1963 that the failure to provide a lawyer for Gideon had violated the Constitution. This far-reaching ruling said:

From the beginning our state and national constitutions and laws have laid great emphasis on procedural and substantive safeguards designed to assure fair trials before impartial tribunals in which every defendant stands equal before the law. This noble ideal cannot be realized if the poor man charged with a crime has to face his accusers without a lawyer to represent him.

In a third major case, Ernesto Miranda appealed to the court after having been convicted of kidnapping and rape in Arizona. During questioning by the police there, he had confessed and signed a written statement—without having been told he had the right to consult a lawyer. In 1966, the Supreme Court reversed his conviction on the grounds that his rights as an accused person had been violated. The court ruled that suspects must be warned by the police that they have a right to keep silent, that anything they say may be used against them, and that they have the right to a lawyer. Since then, these have become known as Miranda warnings, used by police everywhere.

While the court's decisions on this trio of criminal cases profoundly affected the everyday workings of the nation's police and court systems, they had little impact on the great majority of law-abiding citizens. Two other cases—involving school prayers and voting rights—affected all Americans not only at the time of the decisions, but even today.

At issue in the school prayer case was the question of whether it was legal for children in Merrick, New York, to say a brief prayer in school each morning: "Almighty God, we acknowledge our dependence upon Thee, and we beg Thy blessings upon us, our parents, our teachers, and our country."

Five parents thought these twenty-two words were unconstitutional when used in school, and sued to stop the prayers. They lost in the lower courts, which held that the prayer did not violate any constitutional rights as long as it was not compulsory. The parents appealed to the Supreme Court.

In similar earlier cases, the court had barred reading the Bible in public schools at the start of the school day or singing hymns or teaching religion in the schools as a violation of the First Amendment to the Constitution. It had held that the due process clause of the Fourteenth Amendment made the First Amendment binding on the states as well as the federal government, so no state could pass a law or adopt any regulation "respecting an establishment of religion."

Despite arguments by the Merrick school board that the prayers in its schools were voluntary, not compulsory, the Warren Court declared the practice unconstitutional. Prayer in the schools, the court asserted, was wholly inconsistent with the First Amendment's clause, "Congress shall make no law respecting an establishment of religion." School prayers of any sort, the court held, were clearly a religious activity, and the Constitution forbade any public agency from composing "official prayers for any group of American people to recite as part of a religious program carried on by government."

In the furor this ruling aroused, there were calls for constitutional amendments that would permit prayer in the schools. None of these were adopted, but arguments about prayer or silent meditation in the schools have not ceased

Another decision that caused an uproar concerned the unequal size of election districts, giving some voters more weight than others in choosing representatives. For years, the Supreme Court had refused to hear any legal action about setting the size of election districts, saying this was a matter for the individual states.

That changed in the case of *Baker v. Carr* in 1962. Some

Tennessee voters had complained that the unequal size of the legislative districts in their state made their votes count less than others and thus deprived them of the equal protection guaranteed by the Fourteenth Amendment. As an example, they cited several counties with small populations that had greater representation in the state assembly than rapidly growing areas because the districts had not been reapportioned since 1901.

Although the Supreme Court agreed with them, thus for the first time getting involved in the question of local political contests, it left the solution to the lower courts. Within a year, similar suits had been brought in thirty states. The Warren Court generally held to the stand that "the conception of political equality . . . can mean only one thing, one person, one vote."

As a result of the court's decisions in these cases, thousands of districts choosing county, state, and Congressional representatives all had to be redrawn so they contained roughly the same number of voters. Although compliance was fairly rapid, some objectors who claimed that geographic variations should be recognized attempted to promote another constitutional amendment overthrowing the decision. It failed. By the end of the 1960s, most state legislatures had been reapportioned on the basis of the equal population standard.

Chief Justice Warren himself once said he thought his decision that "legislators represent people, not trees or acres" had been the most important contribution of his entire career. Most experts thought, though, that he was being too modest. In the basic textbook on the Supreme Court most law students are required to master, the verdict on Warren's contribution was much broader: "The phrase 'constitutional revolution' seems almost certainly no exaggeration to describe the cumulative effect of the Warren Court's expansive interpretations of the Bill of Rights and the Fourteenth Amendment."

Yet soon after Warren retired at the age of seventy-eight, he offered his own more down-to-earth assessment of what he had achieved. Attending a ceremony at the University of California in 1969, held to celebrate the opening of its new Earl Warren Legal Center, the guest of honor smiled broadly. "You don't have to be a great success in law school to have a building named after you," he said.

Just one other fact about the Warren Court must be added. Toward the end of his tenure, in 1967 President Johnson gave him a new colleague who was also a big, friendly lawyer unafraid of stirring controversy. That year, Thurgood Marshall—the "mastermind" behind the famous *Brown v. the Board of Education,* who had achieved the remarkable record of winning twenty-nine civil rights cases out of the thirty-two he argued before the nation's top tribunal— became the first black justice appointed to serve on the Supreme Court.

14

The Living Constitution

ON ELECTION DAY OF 1972, eleven million young Americans—eighteen, nineteen, and twenty years old—voted for the first time. How that came to happen provides a fine example of the way Congress, the Supreme Court, the state governments, and the nation's people all interact to make the Constitution a living document, which changes to meet new challenges.

The process started with the Voting Rights Act of 1970, essentially a law to extend the rights of black voters in the South. But this was during the Vietnam War, shortly after four students demonstrating for peace at Kent State University in Ohio had been shot and killed by National Guard troops. As a result, thousands of students descended on Washington to protest against the war and to urge that the long-established voting age of twenty-one be lowered.

Surprisingly, they found support from two of the oldest men in Congress. One was the seventy-eight-year-old

Speaker of the House of Representatives, John McCormack. He went to his colleague, Emanuel Celler, the eighty-one-year-old chairman of the House Judiciary Committee. "Manny," he said, "times are changing and the time for the eighteen-year-old vote has come, and we ought to give in as gracefully as possible."

With these two powerful patriarchs pushing for action, Congress acted. The 1970 Voting Rights measure included these words:

> The Congress finds and declares that the imposition and the application of the requirement that a citizen be twenty-one years old as a precondition to voting in any primary or in any election denies and abridges the inherent constitutional rights of citizens eighteen years old but not yet twenty-one years old to vote — a particularly unfair treatment of such citizens in view of the national defense responsibilities imposed on such citizens.

After the bill passed in Congress, President Nixon signed it even though he was concerned about the legality of lowering the voting age by legislation rather than by a constitutional amendment. Moreover, many states objected to any federal regulation of elections within their borders. Two of them, Oregon and Texas, sued the United States to stop enforcement of the new law in the case that became known as *Oregon v. Mitchell*—John Mitchell was then the Attorney General of the United States.

This turned out to be one of the first cases heard before a new Chief Justice, Warren E. Burger of Virginia, who had been appointed on June 23, 1969 to succeed Earl Warren. Concerning *Oregon v. Mitchell* the Burger court was far from unanimous.

Four justices decided that the Congressional action reducing the voting age was valid for all elections, state as well as national. Four others said it exceeded the powers of Congress to set conditions governing all elections, national and state. And one justice held that the law was constitutional as it applied to national elections, which Congress controlled, but unconstitutional for state elections, which were up to the states. The product of all this independent thinking was a five-to-four verdict permitting eighteen-year-olds to vote in national elections, but not in state contests.

The decision posed a terrible problem for election officials all over the nation. With the election of 1972 not far off, would they have to prepare two separate ballots—one for President, the Senate, and the House of Representatives, which every eighteen-and-up voter could cast, and another for governors, mayors, and other state or local officials, to be used only by voters over twenty-one?

It was an impossible situation, solved by fast political action. On March 23, 1971, just three months after the Supreme Court decision, Congress formally proposed the Twenty-sixth Amendment to the Constitution, stating:

The right of citizens of the United States, who are eighteen years of age or older, to vote shall not be denied or abridged by the United States or by any State on account of age.

A record for speed in ratifying an amendment was set by the states, which obviously did not want the confusion of a dual ballot system Within three months after Congress had proposed the amendment, the required thirty-eight states had ratified it. On July 1, 1971, it became part of the Constitution in plenty of time to give all eighteen-, nineteen-, and twenty-year-olds the right to vote for all officials in the 1972 elections.

It was only the fourth time in United States history that

the Constitution had been amended to overturn a Supreme Court decision. The other three instances, involving the Eleventh, the Fourteenth, and the Sixteenth Amendments, have been discussed in earlier chapters. Now it is time to look at some of the proposed amendments that were not adopted.

In the 200-year history of the Constitution, more than 10,000 amendments have been suggested in Congress. Of these, only thirty-three received Congressional approval and were sent to the states for ratification. Just twenty-six of the thirty-three did become part of the Constitution.

Of the other seven proposed but not ratified, the first two were part of the original Bill of Rights considered back in George Washington's Presidency. One of these would have reapportioned seats in Congress and the other restricted salary increases for congressmen. Because they failed to win ratification by a sufficient number of states, it became generally accepted that Congress itself could decide such matters.

Then, in 1810, Congress proposed an amendment that would have deprived any American of United States citizenship upon accepting a title of nobility, pension, payment, or office from any foreign country. However, only twelve states ratified this extension of the constitutional provision barring any officer of the United States from accepting any gift or honor from a foreign country. So the proposal died.

It was fifty years before Congress advanced any other amendment. On March 2, 1861, two days before Abraham Lincoln became President, Congress took a step reflecting the martial tension gripping the capital as a result of the secession of several Southern states. It approved an amendment that would have prohibited any future change in the Constitution abolishing or interfering with slavery. Only two states—Ohio and Maryland—ratified it. Not till after the Civil War ended would the three "war amendments," the Thirteenth, Fourteenth, and Fifteenth, finally end the slavery controversy, constitutionally speaking.

Child labor proved to be another issue it took a long time to resolve from the constitutional standpoint. Around the turn of this century, reformist writers began to publicize some shocking facts about factories employing children as young as five years old. In New York City alone, an estimated 10,000 youngsters worked under terrible conditions, turning out products from paper flowers to shirt collars. The indignation aroused by newspaper stories about boys and girls working in dark, filthy buildings without fire escapes convinced Congress to pass a law forbidding the interstate shipment of any items from a factory or cannery where children less than fourteen worked.

But, in 1918, the Supreme Court declared that law unconstitutional. The following year, Congress tried again to regulate child labor by imposing a tax on the profits of employers of young children. Owing to the prevailing laissez faire philosophy about noninterference with private enterprise, the Supreme Court struck that down, too.

In 1924, Congress responded by proposing an amendment to the Constitution permitting the passage of legislation to limit or even prohibit "the labor of persons under eighteen years of age." Over a period of years, twenty-eight states ratified the Child Labor Amendment—but eighteen other states refused to do so, resulting in its defeat. Nevertheless, its purpose eventually was accomplished because the Supreme Court itself reversed its own very strict interpretation of the Constitution and upheld new laws aimed at protecting young people from unscrupulous employers.

Of all the failed amendments, however, none came closer

to adoption—and caused more controversy—than the ERA of modern times. It was the Equal Rights Amendment, stating:

> Equality of rights under the law shall not be denied or abridged by the United States or by any State on account of sex.

Back in 1920, right after the woman's suffrage amendment became the law of the land, some of its most determined supporters had vowed to press on for a further constitutional guarantee. They wanted to supplement their newly-won right to vote, granted by the Nineteenth Amendment, with another broader ban on every sort of law or practice discriminating against females.

Still, it took a new wave of feminist protest during the 1960s to bring this issue before the wider public. In 1972, Congress recognized the mounting support for the measure by recommending adoption of the Equal Rights Amendment. But it set a time limit of seven years for the process of ratification, just as it had on several previously proposed amendments.

At first, it seemed that the enthusiastic ERA campaign by women's rights groups would easily succeed. By the end of 1972, twenty-two states had ratified the amendment, and the following year eight more states approved it. Then a vigorous countereffort by opponents contending that ERA would radically change the whole fabric of American life began showing results.

Over the next five years, only five more state legislatures voted in favor—giving the pro-ERA forces a score of thirty-five. It proved impossible to win the three additional needed to secure adoption. And so, in 1979, when the seven-year limit expired, the Equal Rights Amendment died.

One other amendment also failed because not enough states ratified it within the time limit set by Congress. Pertaining to the District of Columbia, it would have repealed the Twenty-third Amendment, which gave residents of the district the right to vote for President, and replaced it with a broader amendment allowing capital residents to vote for members of Congress as well. This change, proposed in 1978, had been ratified by only sixteen states during the seven years until 1985, so it, too, died.

Today, hundreds of proposed amendments are at least technically under consideration by various Congressional committees. Most of these represent attempts to reverse decisions of the Supreme Court, while others aim to force Congress to take some action it has been reluctant to take on its own. For instance, dozens of amendments have been introduced to compel the balancing of the federal budget—a feat that has not been accomplished in modern times.

Among the numerous suggested amendments that would overrule a Supreme Court decision strongly opposed by some segment of the population, several involve two of the most highly charged issues of the day. These amendments would, in substance, prohibit abortions or permit prayer in the nation's schools.

But amendments are only one way of changing the Constitution. As we have seen already, the Supreme Court throughout the years has repeatedly changed its interpretation of various clauses in the light of changing conditions as well as changes in the outlook of the justices themselves. While there have been swings back and forth between broad and narrow views about the document's meaning, the trend during this century has generally been toward a broader and broader interpretation.

The Bill of Rights provides a good example of this process.

Today, almost everybody believes that the Bill of Rights guarantees all Americans against any sort of infringement of such basic rights as freedom of speech. But back when it was adopted, there was no doubt that it was aimed specifically at limiting the powers of the national government. Whatever protection people had against infringements by the states was assumed to depend on the constitutions of the individual states.

The first case claiming that a state had wrongfully deprived a citizen of a right guaranteed in the Federal Constitution's Bill of Rights arose in 1832. Then John Marshall's Supreme Court ruled explicitly that the Bill of Rights did not apply to actions by state governments. Not till nearly a century later did the public begin to see evidence of a somewhat roundabout reversal on this basic question.

It was 1925 when the Supreme Court finally declared that the right to free speech could not be abridged by a state. But this direct reversal of previous doctrine rested on the sort of indirect and rather convoluted reasoning only lawyers really appreciate. In effect, the court plucked a few phrases out of the Fourteenth Amendment and used them to justify a new interpretation of the First Amendment.

"We may and do assume," the court said, "that freedom of speech and of the press—which are protected by the First Amendment from abridgement by Congress—are among the personal rights and liberties protected by the due process clause of the Fourteenth Amendment from impairment by the states."

From then on, in one case after another the court arrived at similar decisions regarding other Bill of Rights protections. It ruled that the Fourteenth Amendment guaranteed citizens the right to compensation for property taken by a state and forbade unreasonable searches or seizures by a state. Other constitutional provisions requiring various safeguards of individual rights for suspects arrested by police also were extended to cover state as well as federal actions. While the court never ruled that all the protections of the Bill of Rights applied to the states, it achieved the same result by the process lawyers called "incorporating" the Bill of Rights into the Fourteenth Amendment.

Although most thoughtful observers welcomed the new protections, some insisted that the Supreme Court was going too far in "coddling" those accused of crimes. Other criticism of the court also grew more vocal with the electorate's shift toward a more conservative outlook during the 1980s, when one of President Reagan's closest aides opened an extraordinary public debate about the court. He did so in a 1985 speech that made the front page of the new day's New York *Times*. Its story started:

> *Washington,* July 9—Attorney General Edwin Meese 3d said today that the framers of the Constitution would have found "bizarre" the Supreme Court's recent reaffirmation that the First Amendment requires government to maintain "strict neutrality" toward religion.
>
> "Far too many of the court's opinions, on the whole, have been more policy choices than articulations of long-term constitutional principle," he said in a speech before the American Bar Association. . . .

Meese's blunt words caused a furor. Surprisingly, some of the justices of the Supreme Court broke their traditional silence in the face of criticism and replied with speeches of their own. Justice John Paul Stevens spoke up so vigorously that he, too, made headlines like:

JUSTICE STEVENS, IN RARE CRITICISM, DISPUTES MEESE ON CONSTITUTION

So did Justice William J. Brennan:

BRENNAN OPPOSES LEGAL VIEW URGED BY ADMINISTRATION

The crucial point in this remarkable debate related to the meaning of the words written in the Constitution 200 years earlier. Were these words to be taken literally, two centuries later, in deciding cases before the Supreme Court? Or did the justices have an obligation to adapt them to current problems?

Debating questions like these was not merely an exercise for lawyers, historians, and students. It could affect the daily lives of all Americans. Some of the issues that lay behind the verbal conflict—issues like abortion and compulsory school busing—had already aroused fierce emotions because they touched so deeply on personal matters. Yet the whole range of Supreme Court decisions that had brought on the dissension highlighted the fundamental divergence in political philosophy separating President Reagan's supporters and his opponents.

Thus, the debate was really a battle for public opinion. While awaiting the retirement of some of the aging justices who struck Reagan as too liberal, his friends hoped their criticism might subtly influence the court's decisions even before new Reagan appointees gave it a more conservative cast. That had worked during Franklin Roosevelt's Presidency, when his attacks on a conservative court had produced a move toward a more liberal outlook. Now it was the turn of the conservatives.

As spokesman for the conservative cause, Meese took a strong position in favor of what he called "a jurisprudence of original intention." That meant he thought it was the court's function just to determine the intention of the men who had written the Constitution, and then to apply the same principle as a guide in deciding any contemporary case.

"Those who framed the Constitution chose their words carefully," Meese said. "They debated at great length the most minute points. The language they chose meant something. It is incumbent upon the court to determine what that meaning was." To Meese, the adoption of any other standard meant pouring new meaning into old words, "creating new powers and new rights totally at odds with the logic of our Constitution and its commitment to the rule of law."

Yet the Meese view struck Justice Brennan, who had served twenty-nine years on the Supreme Court, as nonsense. "It is arrogant," he said, "to pretend that from our vantage point we can gauge accurately the intent of the framers" about how to apply the values of 1787 in deciding specific questions arising from vastly changed conditions 200 years later.

The great strength of the Constitution, Brennan contended, was that it remained a living document, growing with the times. He added:

We current justices read the Constitution in the only way we can: as twentieth-century Americans. We look to the history of the time of framing and to the intervening history of interpretation. But the ultimate question must be, what do the words of the text mean in our time? For the genius of the Constitution rests not in any static meaning it might have had in a world that is dead and gone, but in the adaptability of its great principles to cope with current problems and current needs.

How will this great debate end? Although predicting is risky, the record of the past suggests that the Meese view will probably not prevail in the long run. Anybody familiar with the proceedings in Independence Hall back in 1787 is likely to be more impressed by the Brennan argument. For there was no clear common intention among the framers of the Constitution, as earlier chapters have shown, apart from their belief that a new Constitution was necessary for the survival of the young United States.

To achieve agreement, they glossed over many differences, they made major compromises. Their product—the Constitution itself—marked only the beginning of American constitutional history. Over the years, it has been changed by amendments to meet situations the framers could not have imagined. It has grown, too, through decisions of the Supreme Court giving continuity and contemporary force to old words and phrases, fitting them to deal with new problems. The mere fact that the document has survived for two centuries is evidence that it has been adaptable to change and growth.

But as the nation celebrated the two hundredth anniversary of "the miracle at Philadelphia," a disturbing possibility lurked in the background. During the 1980s, a move to convene a second constitutional convention quietly gained strength.

By the terms of Article V of the Constitution, which sets forth the procedure for amending the document, Congress is given the power to propose amendments itself. In addition, though, it is empowered to call a convention to consider amendments "on the application of two-thirds of the several States." Since 1787, no such convention has ever been summoned.

Nor do practical politicians foresee any real likelihood of

another convention, despite quite a bit of maneuvering in this direction. Proponents of several amendments that Congress has been unwilling to propose have managed to secure a surprising amount of support for the untried alternate method. A total of thirty-four states must join in asking Congress to call a new convention—and thirty-two have already adopted motions favoring such a meeting to sponsor an amendment that would compel the balancing of the federal budget.

Also, nineteen states are on record as supporting a convention to propose an amendment that would prohibit abortion, thirteen want an amendment forbidding compulsory school busing, and five an amendment permitting voluntary prayer in the schools. But beyond advocating one or another controversial proposal for amending the Constitution, what harm could any new convention do?

When the original Constitutional Convention met back in 1787, it made its own rules. Instead of following the mandate of the Continental Congress and merely revising the Articles of Confederation, the 1787 convention adopted an entirely new document. Could a modern assemblage follow in its footsteps and adopt a brand-new constitution for the United States?

Of course, the chance of any such overturning of the existing Constitution is extremely slim. Over the past 200 years, Americans have accepted the Constitution as the supreme law of the land and are not likely to approve any major changes in it, much less an entirely new document. But if a new constitutional convention should assemble, who knows what might happen?

Text of the Constitution
of the United States of America

WE THE PEOPLE of the United States, in Order to form a more perfect Union, establish Justice, insure domestic Tranquility, provide for the common defence, promote the general Welfare, and secure the Blessings of Liberty to ourselves and our Posterity, do ordain and establish this Constitution for the United States of America.

ARTICLE I.

SECTION 1. All legislative Powers herein granted shall be vested in a Congress of the United States, which shall consist of a Senate and House of Representatives.

SECTION 2. The House of Representatives shall be composed of Members chosen every second Year by the People of the several States, and the Electors in each State shall have the Qualifications requisite for Electors of the most numerous Branch of the State Legislature.

No Person shall be a Representative who shall not have attained to the Age of twenty-five Years, and been seven Years a Citizen of the United States, and who shall not, when elected, be an Inhabitant of that State in which he shall be chosen.

[Representatives and direct Taxes shall be apportioned among the several States which may be included within this Union, according to their respective Numbers, which shall be determined by adding to the whole Number of free Persons, including those bound to Service for a Term of Years, and excluding Indians not taxed, three fifths of all other Persons.] The actual Enumeration shall be made within three Years after the first Meeting of the Congress of the United States, and within every

[NOTE: Material in brackets has been superseded by subsequent amendments.]

subsequent Term of ten Years, in such Manner as they shall by Law direct. The Number of Representatives shall not exceed one for every thirty Thousand, but each State shall have at Least one Representative; and until such enumeration shall be made, the State of New Hampshire shall be entitled to chuse three, Massachusetts eight, Rhode-Island and Providence Plantations one, Connecticut five, New-York six, New Jersey four, Pennsylvania eight, Delaware one, Maryland six, Virginia ten, North Carolina five, South Carolina five, and Georgia three.

When vacancies happen in the Representation from any State, the Executive Authority thereof shall issue Writs of Election to fill such Vacancies.

The House of Representatives shall chuse their Speaker and other Officers; and shall have the sole Power of Impeachment.

SECTION 3. The Senate of the United States shall be composed of two Senators from each State, [chosen by the Legislature thereof,] for six Years; and each Senator shall have one Vote.

Immediately after they shall be assembled in Consequence of the first Election, they shall be divided as equally as may be into three Classes. The Seats of the Senators of the first Class shall be vacated at the Expiration of the second Year, of the second Class at the Expiration of the fourth Year, and of the third Class at the Expiration of the sixth Year, so that one-third may be chosen every second Year; [and if Vacancies happen by Resignation, or otherwise, during the Recess of the Legislature of any State, the Executive thereof may make temporary Appointments until the next Meeting of the Legislature, which shall then fill such Vacancies.]

No Person shall be a Senator who shall not have attained to the Age of thirty Years, and been nine Years a Citizen of the United States, and who shall not, when elected, be an Inhabitant of that State for which he shall be chosen.

The Vice President of the United States shall be President of the Senate, but shall have no Vote, unless they be equally divided.

The Senate shall chuse their other Officers, and also a President pro tempore, in the Absence of the Vice President, or when he shall exercise the Office of President of the United States.

The Senate shall have the sole Power to try all Impeachments. When sitting for that Purpose, they shall be on Oath or Affirmation. When the President of the United States is tried, the Chief Justice shall preside: And no Person shall be convicted without the Concurrence of two thirds of the Members present.

Judgment in Cases of Impeachment shall not extend further than to removal from Office, and disqualification to hold and enjoy any Office of honor, Trust or Profit under the United States: but the Party convicted shall nevertheless be liable and subject to Indictment, Trial, Judgment and Punishment, according to Law.

SECTION 4. The Times, Places and Manner of holding Elections for Senators and Representatives shall be prescribed in each State by the Legislature thereof; but the Congress may at any time by Law make or alter such Regulations, except as to the Place of Chusing Senators.

The Congress shall assemble at least once in every Year, and such Meeting shall [be on the first Monday in December,] unless they shall by Law appoint a different Day.

SECTION 5. Each House shall be the Judge of the Elections, Returns and Qualifications of its own Members, and a Majority of each shall constitute a Quorum to do Business; but a smaller number may adjourn from day to day, and may be authorized to compel the Attendance of absent Members, in such Manner, and under such Penalties as each House may provide.

Each House may determine the Rules of its Proceedings, punish its Members for disorderly Behavior, and, with the Concurrence of two thirds, expel a Member.

Each House shall keep a Journal of its Proceedings, and from time to time publish the same, excepting such Parts as may in their Judgment require Secrecy; and the Yeas and Nays of the Members of either House on any question shall, at the Desire of one fifth of those Present, be entered on the Journal.

Neither House, during the Session of Congress, shall, without the Consent of the other, adjourn for more than three days, nor to any other Place than that in which the two Houses shall be sitting.

SECTION 6. The Senators and Representatives shall receive a Compensation for their Services, to be ascertained by Law, and paid out of the Treasury of the United States. They shall in all Cases, except Treason, Felony and Breach of the Peace, be privileged from Arrest during their Attendance at the Session of their respective Houses, and in going to and returning from the same; and for any Speech or Debate in either House, they shall not be questioned in any other Place.

No Senator or Representative shall, during the Time for which he was elected, be appointed to any civil Office under the Authority of the United States, which shall have been created, or the Emoluments whereof shall have been encreased during such time; and no Person holding any Office under the United States, shall be a Member of either House during his Continuance in Office.

SECTION 7. All Bills for raising Revenue shall originate in the House of Representatives; but the Senate may propose or concur with Amendments as on other Bills.

Every Bill which shall have passed the House of Representatives and the Senate, shall, before it become a Law, be presented to the President of the United States; If he approve he shall sign it, but if not he shall return it, with his Objections to that House in which it shall have originated, who shall enter the Objections at large on their Journal, and proceed to reconsider it. If after such Reconsideration two thirds of that House shall agree to pass the Bill, it shall be sent, together with the Objections, to the other House, by which it shall likewise be reconsidered, and if approved by two thirds of that House, it shall become a Law. But in all such Cases the Votes of both Houses shall be determined by Yeas and Nays, and the Names of the Persons voting for and against the Bill shall be entered on the Journal of each House respectively. If any Bill shall not be returned by the President within ten Days (Sundays excepted) after it shall have been presented to him, the Same shall be a Law, in like Manner as if he had signed it, unless the Congress by their Adjournment prevent its Return, in which Case it shall not be a Law.

Every Order, Resolution, or Vote to which the Concurrence of the Senate and House of Representatives may be necessary (except on a question of Adjournment) shall be presented to the President of the United States; and before the Same shall take Effect, shall be approved by him, or being disapproved by him, shall be repassed by two thirds of the Senate and House of Representatives, according to the Rules and Limitations prescribed in the Case of a Bill.

SECTION 8. The Congress shall have Power To lay and collect Taxes, Duties, Imposts and Excises, to pay the Debts and provide for the common Defense and general Welfare of the United States; but all Duties, Imposts and Excises shall be uniform throughout the United States;

To borrow Money on the credit of the United States;

To regulate Commerce with foreign Nations, and among the several States, and with the Indian Tribes;

To establish an uniform Rule of Naturalization, and uniform Laws on the subject of Bankruptcies throughout the United States;

To coin Money, regulate the Value thereof, and of foreign Coin, and fix the Standard of Weights and Measures;

To provide for the Punishment of counterfeiting the Securities and current Coin of the United States;

To establish Post Offices and post Roads;

To promote the Progress of Science and useful Arts, by securing for limited Times to Authors and Inventors the exclusive Right to their respective Writings and Discoveries;

To constitute Tribunals inferior to the Supreme Court;

To define and punish Piracies and Felonies committed on the high Seas, and Offenses against the Law of Nations;

To declare War, grant Letters of Marque and Reprisal, and make Rules concerning Captures on Land and Water;

To raise and support Armies, but no Appropriation of Money to that Use shall be for a longer Term than two Years;

To provide and maintain a Navy;

To make Rules for the Government and Regulation of the land and naval Forces;

To provide for calling forth the Militia to execute the Laws of the Union, suppress Insurrections and repel Invasions;

To provide for organizing, arming, and disciplining the Militia, and for governing such Part of them as may be employed in the Service of the United States, reserving to the States respectively, the Appointment of the Officers, and the Authority of training the Militia according to the discipline prescribed by Congress;

To exercise exclusive Legislation in all Cases whatsoever, over such District (not exceeding ten Miles square) as may, by Cession of particular States, and the Acceptance of Congress, become the Seat of Government of the United States, and to exercise like Authority over all Places purchased by the Consent of the Legislature of the State in which the Same shall be, for the Erection of Forts, Magazines, Arsenals, dock-Yards, and other needful Buildings;—And

To make all Laws which shall be necessary and proper for carrying into Execution the foregoing Powers, and all other Powers vested by this Constitution in the Government of the United States, or in any Department or Officer thereof.

SECTION 9. The Migration or Importation of such Persons as any of the States now existing shall think proper to admit, shall not be prohibited by the Congress prior to the Year one thousand eight hundred and eight, but a tax or duty may be imposed on such Importation, not exceeding ten dollars for each Person.

The privilege of the Writ of Habeas Corpus shall not be suspended, unless when in Cases of Rebellion or Invasion the public Safety may require it.

No Bill of Attainder or ex post facto Law shall be passed.

No capitation, or other direct, Tax shall be laid, unless in Proportion to the Census or Enumeration herein before directed to be taken.

No Tax or Duty shall be laid on Articles exported from any State.

No Preference shall be given by any Regulation of Commerce or Revenue to the Ports of one State over those of another: nor shall Vessels bound to, or from, one State, be obliged to enter, clear, or pay Duties in another.

No Money shall be drawn from the Treasury, but in Consequence of Appropriations made by Law; and a regular Statement and Account of the Receipts and Expenditures of all public Money shall be published from time to time.

No Title of Nobility shall be granted by the United States: And no Person holding any Office of Profit or Trust under them, shall, without the Consent of the Congress, accept of any present, Emolument, Office, or Title, of any kind whatever, from any King, Prince, or foreign State.

SECTION 10. No State shall enter into any Treaty, Alliance, or Confederation; grant Letters of Marque and Reprisal; coin Money; emit Bills of Credit; make any Thing but gold and silver Coin a Tender in Payment of Debts; pass any Bill of Attainder, ex post facto Law, or Law impairing the Obligation of Contracts, or grant any Title of Nobility.

No State shall, without the consent of the Congress, lay any Imposts or Duties on Imports or Exports, except what may be absolutely necessary for executing its inspection Laws: and the net Produce of all Duties and Imposts, laid by any State on Imports or Exports, shall be for the Use of the Treasury of the United States; and all such Laws shall be subject to the Revision and Controul of the Congress.

No State shall, without the Consent of Congress, lay any duty of Tonnage, keep Troops, or Ships of War in time of Peace, enter into any Agreement or Compact with another State, or with a foreign Power, or engage in War, unless actually invaded, or in such imminent Danger as will not admit of delay.

ARTICLE II.

SECTION 1. The executive Power shall be vested in a President of the United States of America. He shall hold his Office during the Term of four Years, and, together with the Vice-President, chosen for the same Term, be elected, as follows

Each State shall appoint, in such Manner as the Legislature thereof may direct, a Number of Electors, equal to the whole Number of Senators and Representatives to which the State may be entitled in the Congress: but no Senator or Representative, or Person holding an Office of Trust or Profit under the United States, shall be appointed an Elector.

[The Electors shall meet in their respective States, and vote by Ballot for two persons, of whom one at least shall not be an Inhabitant of the same State with themselves. And they shall make a List of all the Persons voted for, and of the Number of Votes for each; which List they shall sign and certify, and transmit sealed to the Seat of Government of the United States, directed to the President of the Senate. The President of the Senate shall, in the Presence of the Senate and House of Representatives, open all the Certificates, and the Votes shall then be counted. The Person having the greatest Number of Votes shall be the President, if such Number be a Majority of the whole Number of Electors appointed; and if there be more than one who have such Majority, and have an equal Number of Votes, then the House of Representatives shall immediately chuse by Ballot one of them for President; and if no Person have a Majority, then from the five highest on the List the said House shall in like Manner chuse the President. But in chusing the President, the Votes shall be taken by States, the Representation from each State having one Vote; a quorum for this Purpose shall consist of a Member or Members from two-thirds of the States, and a Majority of all the States shall be necessary to a Choice. In every Case, after the Choice of the President, the Person having the greatest Number of Votes of the Electors shall be the Vice President. But if there should remain two or more who have equal Votes, the Senate shall chuse from them by Ballot the Vice-President.]

The Congress may determine the Time of chusing the Electors, and the Day on which they shall give their Votes; which Day shall be the same throughout the United States.

No Person except a natural born Citizen, or a Citizen of the United States, at the time of the Adoption of this Constitution, shall be eligible to the Office of President; neither shall any Person be eligible to that Office who shall not have attained to the Age of thirty-five Years, and been fourteen Years a Resident within the United States.

[In Case of the Removal of the President from Office, or of his Death, Resignation, or Inability to discharge the Powers and Duties of the said Office, the same shall devolve on the Vice President, and the Congress may by Law, provide for the Case of Removal, Death, Resignation or Inability, both of the President and Vice President, declaring what Officer shall then act as President, and such Officer shall act accordingly, until the Disability be removed, or a President shall be elected.]

The President shall, at stated Times, receive for his Services, a Compensation, which shall neither be encreased nor diminished during the Period for which he shall have been elected, and he shall not receive within that Period any other Emolument from the United States, or any of them.

Before he enter on the Execution of his Office, he shall take the following Oath or Affirmation:—"I do solemnly swear (or affirm) that I will faithfully execute the Office of President of the United States, and will to the best of my Ability, preserve, protect and defend the Constitution of the United States."

SECTION 2. The President shall be Commander in Chief of the Army and Navy of the United States, and of the Militia of the several States, when called into the actual Service of the United States; he may require the Opinion in writing, of the principal Officer in each of the executive Departments, upon any subject relating to the Duties of their respective Offices, and he shall have Power to Grant Reprieves and Pardons for Offenses against the United States, except in Cases of Impeachment.

He shall have Power, by and with the Advice and Consent of the Senate, to make Treaties, provided two-thirds of the Senators present concur; and he shall nominate, and by and with the Advice and Consent of the Senate, shall appoint Ambassadors, other public Ministers and Consuls, Judges of the supreme Court, and all other Officers of the United States, whose Appointments are not herein otherwise provided for, and which shall be established by Law: but the Congress may by Law vest the Appointment of such inferior Officers, as they think proper, in the President alone, in the Courts of Law, or in the Heads of Departments.

The President shall have Power to fill up all Vacancies that may happen during the Recess of the Senate, by granting Commissions which shall expire at the End of their next Session.

SECTION 3. He shall from time to time give to the Congress Information of the State of the Union, and recommend to their Consideration such Measures as he shall judge necessary and expedient; he may, on extraordinary Occasions, convene both Houses, or either of them, and in Case of Disagreement between them, with Respect to the Time of Adjournment, he may adjourn them to such Time as he shall think proper; he shall receive Ambassadors and other public Ministers; he shall take Care that the Laws be faithfully executed, and shall Commission all the Officers of the United States.

SECTION 4. The President, Vice President and all civil Officers of the United States, shall be removed from Office on Impeachment for, and Conviction of, Treason, Bribery, or other high Crimes and Misdemeanors.

ARTICLE III.

SECTION 1. The judicial Power of the United States, shall be vested in one supreme Court, and in such inferior Courts as the Congress may from time to time ordain and establish. The Judges, both of the supreme and inferior Courts, shall hold their Offices during good Behaviour, and shall, at stated Times, receive for their Services, a Compensation, which shall not be diminished during their Continuance in Office.

SECTION 2. The judicial Power shall extend to all Cases, in Law and Equity, arising under this Constitution, the Laws of the United States, and Treaties made, or which shall be made, under their Authority;—to all Cases affecting Ambassadors, other public Ministers and Consuls;—to all Cases of admiralty and maritime Jurisdiction;—to Controversies to which the United States shall be a Party;—to Controversies between two or more States;—between a State and Citizens of another State;—between Citizens of different States;—between Citizens of the same State claiming Lands under Grants of different States, and between a State, or the Citizens thereof, and foreign States, Citizens or Subjects.

In all Cases affecting Ambassadors, other public Ministers and Consuls, and those in which a State shall be a Party, the supreme Court shall have original Jurisdiction. In all the other cases before mentioned, the supreme Court shall have appellate Jurisdiction, both as to Law and Fact, with such Exceptions, and under such Regulations as the Congress shall make.

The Trial of all Crimes, except in Cases of Impeachment, shall be by Jury; and such Trial shall be held in the State where the said Crimes shall have been committed; but when not committed within any State, the Trial shall be at such Place or Places as the Congress may by Law have directed.

SECTION 3. Treason against the United States, shall consist only in levying War against them, or in adhering to their Enemies, giving them Aid and Comfort. No Person shall be convicted of Treason unless on the Testimony of two Witnesses to the same overt Act, or on Confession in open Court.

The Congress shall have Power to declare the Punishment of Treason, but no Attainder of Treason shall work Corruption of Blood, or Forfeiture except during the Life of the Person attainted.

ARTICLE IV.

SECTION 1. Full Faith and Credit shall be given in each State to the public Acts, Records, and judicial Proceedings of every other State. And the Congress may by general Laws prescribe the Manner in which such Acts, Records and Proceedings shall be proved, and the Effect thereof.

SECTION 2. The Citizens of each State shall be entitled to all Privileges and Immunities of Citizens in the several States.

A Person charged in any State with Treason, Felony, or other Crime, who shall flee from Justice, and be found in another State, shall, on demand of the executive Authority of the State from which he fled, be delivered up, to be removed to the State having Jurisdiction of the Crime.

[No Person held to Service or Labour in one State, under the Laws thereof, escaping into another, shall, in Consequence of any Law or Regulation therein, be discharged from such Service or Labour, but shall be delivered up on Claim of the Party to whom such Service or Labour may be due.]

SECTION 3. New States may be admitted by the Congress into this Union; but no new State shall be formed or erected within the Jurisdiction of any other State; nor any State be formed by the Junction of two or more States, or parts of States, without the Consent of the Legislatures of the States concerned as well as of the Congress.

The Congress shall have Power to dispose of and make all needful Rules and Regulations respecting the Territory or other Property belonging to the United States; and nothing in this Constitution shall be so construed as to Prejudice any Claims of the United States, or of any particular State.

SECTION 4. The United States shall guarantee to every State in this Union a Republican Form of Government, and shall protect each of them against Invasion; and on Application of the Legislature, or of the Executive (when the Legislature cannot be convened) against domestic Violence.

ARTICLE V.

The Congress, whenever two-thirds of both Houses shall deem it necessary, shall propose Amendments to this Constitution, or, on the Application of the Legislatures of two-thirds of the several States, shall call a Convention for proposing Amendments, which, in either Case, shall be valid to all Intents and Purposes, as Part of this Constitution, when ratified by the Legislatures of three-fourths of the several States, or by Conventions in three-fourths thereof, as the one or the other Mode of Ratification may be proposed by the Congress; Provided that no Amendment which may be made prior to the Year One thousand eight hundred and eight shall in any Manner affect the first and fourth Clauses in the Ninth Section of the first Article; and that no State, without its Consent, shall be deprived of its equal Suffrage in the Senate.

ARTICLE VI.

All Debts contracted and Engagements entered into, before the Adoption of this Constitution, shall be as valid against the United States under this Constitution, as under the Confederation.

This Constitution, and the Laws of the United States which shall be made in Pursuance thereof; and all Treaties made, or which shall be made, under the Authority of the United States, shall be the supreme Law of the Land; and the Judges in every State shall be bound thereby, any Thing in the Constitution or Laws of any State to the contrary notwithstanding.

The Senators and Representatives before mentioned, and the Members of the several State Legislatures, and all executive and judicial Officers, both of the United States and of the several States, shall be bound by Oath or Affirmation, to support this Constitution; but no religious Test shall ever be required as a Qualification to any Office or public Trust under the United States.

ARTICLE VII.

The Ratification of the Conventions of nine States shall be sufficient for the Establishment of this Constitution between the States so ratifying the Same.

DONE in Convention by the Unanimous Consent of the States present the Seventeenth Day of September in the Year of our Lord one thousand seven hundred and Eighty seven and of the Independence of the United States of America the Twelfth.

In Witness whereof We have hereunto subscribed our Names.

GO WASHINGTON
Presidt and deputy from Virginia

New Hampshire.

JOHN LANGDON
NICHOLAS GILMAN

Massachusetts.

NATHANIEL GORHAM
RUFUS KING

New Jersey.

WIL: LIVINGSTON
DAVID BREARLEY.
WM PATERSON.
JONA: DAYTON

Connecticut.

WM SAML JOHNSON
ROGER SHERMAN

New York.

ALEXANDER HAMILTON

Maryland.

JAMES MCHENRY
DANL CARROL
DAN: of ST THOS JENIFER

Pennsylvania.

B FRANKLIN
ROBT. MORRIS
THOS. FITZSIMONS
JAMES WILSON
THOMAS MIFFLIN
GEO. CLYMER
JARED INGERSOLL
GOUV MORRIS

Delaware.

GEO: READ
JOHN DICKINSON
JACO: BROOM
GUNNING BEDFORD jun
RICHARD BASSETT

Virginia.

JOHN BLAIR—
JAMES MADISON JR.

North Carolina.

WM BLOUNT
HU WILLIAMSON
RICHD DOBBS SPAIGHT.

South Carolina.

J. RUTLEDGE
CHARLES PINCKNEY
CHARLES COTESWORTH PINCKNEY
PIERCE BUTLER

Georgia.

WILLIAM FEW
ABR BALDWIN

Attest:

WILLIAM JACKSON, *Secretary.*

ARTICLES IN ADDITION TO, AND AMENDMENT OF, THE CONSTITUTION
OF THE UNITED STATES OF AMERICA, PROPOSED BY CONGRESS, AND
RATIFIED BY THE LEGISLATURES OF THE SEVERAL STATES, PURSUANT
TO THE FIFTH ARTICLE OF THE ORIGINAL CONSTITUTION.

AMENDMENT I

Congress shall make no law respecting an establishment of religion, or
prohibiting the free exercise thereof; or abridging the freedom of speech,
or of the press; or the right of the people peaceably to assemble, and to
petition the Government for a redress of grievances.

AMENDMENT II

A well regulated Militia, being necessary to the security of a free State,
the right of the people to keep and bear Arms, shall not be infringed.

AMENDMENT III

No Soldier shall, in time of peace be quartered in any house, without the consent of the Owner, nor in time of war, but in a manner to be prescribed by law.

AMENDMENT IV

The right of the people to be secure in their persons, houses, papers, and effects, against unreasonable searches and seizures, shall not be violated, and no Warrants shall issue, but upon probable cause, supported by Oath or affirmation, and particularly describing the place to be searched, and the persons or things to be seized.

AMENDMENT V

No person shall be held to answer for a capital, or otherwise infamous crime, unless on a presentment or indictment of a Grand Jury, except in cases arising in the land or naval forces, or in the Militia, when in actual service in time of War or public danger; nor shall any person be subject for the same offence to be twice put in jeopardy of life or limb; nor shall be compelled in any criminal case to be a witness against himself, nor be deprived of life, liberty, or property, without due process of law; nor shall private property be taken for public use, without just compensation.

AMENDMENT VI

In all criminal prosecutions, the accused shall enjoy the right to a speedy and public trial, by an impartial jury of the State and district wherein the crime shall have been committed, which district shall have been previously ascertained by law, and to be informed of the nature and cause of the accusation; to be confronted with the witnesses against him; to have compulsory process for obtaining witnesses in his favor, and to have the Assistance of Counsel for his defence.

AMENDMENT VII

In suits at common law, where the value in controversy shall exceed twenty dollars, the right of trial by jury shall be preserved, and no fact tried by a jury, shall be otherwise reexamined in any Court of the United States, than according to the rules of the common law.

AMENDMENT VIII

Excessive bail shall not be required, nor excessive fines imposed, nor cruel and unusual punishments inflicted.

AMENDMENT IX

The enumeration in the Constitution, of certain rights, shall not be construed to deny or disparage others retained by the people.

AMENDMENT X

The powers not delegated to the United States by the Constitution, nor prohibited by it to the States, are reserved to the States respectively, or to the people.

AMENDMENT XI

The Judicial power of the United States shall not be construed to extend to any suit in law or equity, commenced or prosecuted against one of the United States by Citizens of another State, or by Citizens or Subjects of any Foreign State.

AMENDMENT XII

The Electors shall meet in their respective states and vote by ballot for President and Vice-President, one of whom, at least, shall not be an inhabitant of the same state with themselves; they shall name in their ballots the person voted for as President, and in distinct ballots the person voted for as Vice-President, and they shall make distinct lists of all persons voted for as President, and of all persons voted for as Vice-President, and of the number of votes for each, which lists they shall sign and certify, and transmit sealed to the seat of the government of the United States, directed to the President of the Senate;—The President of the Senate shall, in presence of the Senate and House of Representatives, open all the certificates and the votes shall then be counted;—The person having the greatest number of votes for President, shall be the President, if such number be a majority of the whole number of Electors appointed; and if no person have such majority, then from the persons having the highest numbers not exceeding three on the list of those voted for as President, the House of Representatives shall choose immediately, by ballot, the President. But in choosing the President, the votes shall be taken by states, the representation from each state having one vote; a quorum for this purpose shall consist of a member or members from two-thirds of the states, and a majority of all the states shall be necessary to a choice. [And if the House of Representatives shall not choose a President whenever the right of choice shall devolve upon them, before the fourth day of March next following, then the Vice-President shall act as President, as in the case of the death or other constitutional disability of the President.—]The person having the greatest number of votes as Vice-President, shall be the Vice President, if such number be a majority of the whole number of Electors appointed, and if no person have a majority, then from the two highest numbers on the list, the Senate shall choose the Vice-President; a quorum for the purpose shall consist of two-thirds of the whole number of Senators, and a majority of the whole number shall be necessary to a choice. But no person constitutionally ineligible to the office of President shall be eligible to that of Vice-President of the United States.

AMENDMENT XIII

SECTION 1. Neither slavery nor involuntary servitude, except as a punishment for crime whereof the party shall have been duly convicted, shall exist within the United States, or any place subject to their jurisdiction.

SECTION 2. Congress shall have power to enforce this article by appropriate legislation.

AMENDMENT XIV

SECTION 1. All persons born or naturalized in the United States, and subject to the jurisdiction thereof, are citizens of the United States and of the State wherein they reside. No State shall make or enforce any law which shall abridge the privileges or immunities of citizens of the United States; nor shall any State deprive any person of life, liberty, or property, without due process of law; nor deny to any person within its jurisdiction the equal protection of the laws.

SECTION 2. Representatives shall be apportioned among the several States according to their respective numbers, counting the whole number of persons in each State, excluding Indians not taxed. But when the right to vote at any election for the choice of electors for President and Vice-President of the United States, Representatives in Congress, the Executive and Judicial officers of a State, or the members of the Legislature thereof, is denied to any of the male inhabitants of such State, being twenty-one years of age, and citizens of the United States, or in any way abridged, except for participation in rebellion, or other crime, the basis of representation therein shall be reduced in the proportion which the number of such male citizens shall bear to the whole number of male citizens twenty-one years of age in such State.

SECTION 3. No person shall be a Senator or Representative in Congress, or elector of President and Vice-President, or hold any office, civil or military, under the United States, or under any State, who, having previously taken an oath, as a member of Congress, or as an officer of the United States, or as a member of any State legislature, or as an executive or judicial officer of any State, to support the Constitution of the United States, shall have engaged in insurrection or rebellion against the same, or given aid or comfort to the enemies thereof. But Congress may by a vote of two-thirds of each House, remove such disability.

SECTION 4. The validity of the public debt of the United States, authorized by law, including debts incurred for payment of pensions and bounties for services in suppressing insurrection or rebellion, shall not be questioned. But neither the United States nor any State shall assume or pay any debt or obligation incurred in aid of insurrection or rebellion against the United States, or any claim for the loss or emancipation of any slave; but all such debts, obligations and claims shall be held illegal and void.

SECTION 5. The Congress shall have power to enforce, by appropriate legislation, the provisions of this article.

AMENDMENT XV

SECTION 1. The right of citizens of the United States to vote shall not be denied or abridged by the United States or by any State on account of race, color, or previous condition of servitude—

SECTION 2. The Congress shall have power to enforce this article by appropriate legislation.

AMENDMENT XVI

The Congress shall have power to lay and collect taxes on incomes, from whatever source derived, without apportionment among the several States, and without regard to any census or enumeration.

AMENDMENT XVII

The Senate of the United States shall be composed of two Senators from each State, elected by the people thereof, for six years; and each Senator shall have one vote. The electors in each State shall have the qualifications requisite for electors of the most numerous branch of the State legislatures.

When vacancies happen in the representation of any State in the Senate, the executive authority of such State shall issue writs of election to fill such vacancies: *Provided*, That the legislature of any State may empower the executive thereof to make temporary appointments until the people fill the vacancies by election as the legislature may direct.

This amendment shall not be so construed as to affect the election or term of any Senator chosen before it becomes valid as part of the Constitution.

AMENDMENT XVIII

[SECTION 1. After one year from the ratification of this article the manufacture, sale, or transportation of intoxicating liquors within, the importation thereof into, or the exportation thereof from the United States and all territory subject to the jurisdiction thereof for beverage purposes is hereby prohibited.

[SECTION 2. The Congress and the several States shall have concurrent power to enforce this article by appropriate legislation.

[SECTION 3. This article shall be inoperative unless it shall have been ratified as an amendment to the Constitution by the legislatures of the several States as provided in the Constitution, within seven years from the date of the submission hereof to the States by the Congress.]

AMENDMENT XIX

The right of citizens of the United States to vote shall not be denied or abridged by the United States or by any State on account of sex.

Congress shall have power to enforce this article by appropriate legislation.

AMENDMENT XX

SECTION 1. The terms of the President and Vice President shall end at noon on the 20th day of January, and the terms of Senators and Representatives at noon on the 3d day of January, of the years in which such terms would have ended if this article had not been ratified; and the terms of their successors shall then begin.

SECTION 2. The Congress shall assemble at least once in every year, and such meeting shall begin at noon on the 3d day of January, unless they shall by law appoint a different day.

SECTION 3. If, at the time fixed for the beginning of the term of the President, the President elect shall have died, the Vice President elect shall become President. If a President shall not have been chosen before the time fixed for the beginning of his term, or if the President elect shall have failed to qualify, then the Vice President elect shall act as President until a President shall have qualified; and the Congress may by law provide for the case wherein neither a President elect nor a Vice President elect shall have qualified, declaring who shall then act as President, or the manner in which one who is to act shall be selected, and such person shall act accordingly until a President or Vice President shall have qualified.

SECTION 4. The Congress may by law provide for the case of the death of any of the persons from whom the House of Representatives may choose a President whenever the right of choice shall have devolved upon them, and for the case of the death of any of the persons from whom the Senate may choose a Vice President whenever the right of choice shall have devolved upon them.

SECTION 5. Sections 1 and 2 shall take effect on the 15th day of October following the ratification of this article.

SECTION 6. This article shall be inoperative unless it shall have been ratified as an amendment to the Constitution by the legislatures of three-fourths of the several States within seven years from the date of its submission.

AMENDMENT XXI

SECTION 1. The eighteenth article of amendment to the Constitution of the United States is hereby repealed.

SECTION 2. The transportation or importation into any State, Territory, or possession of the United States for delivery or use therein of intoxicating liquors, in violation of the laws thereof, is hereby prohibited.

SECTION 3. This article shall be inoperative unless it shall have been ratified as an amendment to the Constitution by conventions in the several States, as provided in the Constitution, within seven years from the date of the submission hereof to the States by the Congress.

AMENDMENT XXII

SECTION 1. No person shall be elected to the office of the President more than twice, and no person who has held the office of President, or acted as President, for more than two years of a term to which some other person was elected President shall be elected to the office of President more than once. But this Article shall not apply to any person holding the office of President when this Article was proposed by the Congress, and shall not prevent any person who may be holding the office of President, or acting as President, during the term within which this Article becomes operative from holding the office of President or acting as President during the remainder of such term.

SECTION 2. This article shall be inoperative unless it shall have been ratified as an amendment to the Constitution by the legislatures of three-fourths of the several States within seven years from the date of its submission to the States by the Congress.

AMENDMENT XXIII

SECTION 1. The District constituting the seat of Government of the United States shall appoint in such manner as the Congress may direct:

A number of electors of President and Vice President equal to the whole number of Senators and Representatives in Congress to which the District would be entitled if it were a State, but in no event more than the least populous State; they shall be in addition to those appointed by the States, but they shall be considered, for the purposes of the election of President and Vice President, to be electors appointed by a State; and they shall meet in the District and perform such duties as provided by the twelfth article of amendment.

SECTION 2. The Congress shall have the power to enforce this article by appropriate legislation.

AMENDMENT XXIV

SECTION 1. The right of citizens of the United States to vote in any primary or other election for President or Vice President, for electors for President or Vice President, or for Senator or Representative in Congress, shall not be denied or abridged by the United States or any State by reason of failure to pay any poll tax or other tax.

SECTION 2. The Congress shall have the power to enforce this article by appropriate legislation.

AMENDMENT XXV

SECTION 1. In case of the removal of the President from office or of his death or resignation, the Vice President shall become President.

SECTION 2. Whenever there is a vacancy in the office of the Vice President, the President shall nominate a Vice President who shall take office upon confirmation by a majority vote of both Houses of Congress.

SECTION 3. Whenever the President transmits to the President pro tempore of the Senate and the Speaker of the House of Representatives his written declaration that he is unable to discharge the powers and duties of his office, and until he transmits to them a written declaration to the contrary, such powers and duties shall be discharged by the Vice President as Acting President.

SECTION 4. Whenever the Vice President and a majority of either the principal officers of the executive departments or of such other body as Congress may by law provide, transmit to the President pro tempore of the Senate and the Speaker of the House of Representatives their written declaration that the President is unable to discharge the powers and duties of his office, the Vice President shall immediately assume the powers and duties of the office as Acting President.

Thereafter, when the President transmits to the President pro tempore of the Senate and the Speaker of the House of Representatives his written declaration that no inability exists, he shall resume the powers and duties of his office unless the Vice President and a majority of either the principal officers of the executive department or of such other body as Congress may by law provide, transmit within four days to the President pro tempore of the Senate and the Speaker of the House of Representatives their written declaration that the President is unable to discharge the powers and duties of his office. Thereupon Congress shall decide the issue, assembling within forty-eight hours for that purpose if not in session. If the Congress, within twenty-one days after receipt of the latter written declaration, or, if Congress is not in session, within twenty-one days after Congress is required to assemble, determines by two-thirds vote of both Houses that the President is unable to discharge the powers and duties of his office, the Vice President shall continue to discharge the same as Acting President; otherwise, the President shall resume the powers and duties of his office.

AMENDMENT XXVI

SECTION 1. The right of citizens of the United States, who are eighteen years of age or older, to vote shall not be denied or abridged by the United States or by any State on account of age.

SECTION 2. The Congress shall have power to enforce this article by appropriate legislation.

A Note on Sources and Bibliography

Our research for this book started at Independence Hall in Philadelphia, where we found much helpful guidance from the resident historians on the staff of the National Park Service—and also were privileged to use their specialized library containing a wealth of material concerning the Constitution. Then, thanks to friends who are lawyers, we consulted many basic texts and commentaries about constitutional issues during the past 200 years.

But the sort of literature intended for historians or members of the legal profession makes rather heavy going for the general reader. So we suggest that anyone wishing to find out more than we have been able to include in our short "biography" of the Constitution should, if possible, visit the Independence Hall National Historical Park in Philadelphia. Besides providing a stirring sense that the great Constitutional Convention of 1787 really happened, the actual setting has been embellished with a number of impressive exhibits.

In addition, here is a list of books or pamphlets we can recommend as both reliable and readable:

Boler, Paul F., Jr. *Presidential Campaigns*. New York: Oxford University Press, 1984.

Bowen, Catherine Drinker. *Miracle at Philadelphia*. Boston: Little, Brown, 1966.

Commager, Henry Steele. *The Great Constitution*. Indianapolis: Bobbs-Merrill, 1961.

Ferris, Robert G., ed. *Signers of the Constitution*. Washington: National Park Service, 1976.

Friendly, Fred W., and Martha J.H. Eliot. *The Constitution: That Delicate Balance*. New York: Random House, 1984.

Garraty, John A., ed. *Quarrels That Have Shaped the Constitution*. New York: Harper & Row, 1964.

Mitchell, Broadus. *A Biography of the Constitution*. New York: Oxford University Press, 1964.

*National Archives and Record Service. *The Formation of the Union*. Washington, D.C.: National Archives and Record Service, 1970.

*——. *A More Perfect Union: The Making of the United States Constitution*. Washington, D.C.: National Archives and Record Service, 1978.

*——. *The Story of the Bill of Rights*. Washington, D.C.: National Archives and Record Service, 1980.

Rossiter, Clinton. *1787 The Grand Convention*. New York: Macmillan, 1966.

Van Doren, Carl. *The Great Revolution*. New York: Viking, 1948.

---

*These books can be ordered by writing to Publications Sales Branch (NEPS), National Archives, Washington, D.C. 20408.

Index